A message from Rick Stein

"It's great reading these books – 'Breakfast' and 'Brunch' – they are amusing as well as having some lovely recipes. Hugo has a strange sense of humour and some of these dishes are rather bizarre… Fried worms is typical of him and the Spicy Beef Burritos must be famous for their lingering afterburn, right up my street as it happens. Indeed I'm going to make Hugo's fruit salad dressing with a dash of red chilli powder like they do in Vera Cruz. This reminds me of the most bizarre breakfast I had early one morning in Mexico, a cup of hot chocolate and cinnamon and a little bag of freshly fried grasshoppers with salt and chilli outside the Benito Juárez Market in Oaxaca".

Best wishes

Rick.

To Phil!
Best of Brunch
Hugo

ISBN & Publishing details

First published in Great Britain by:
Breakfast Book Ltd. Woodlands Country House, Treator, Padstow PL28 8RU

ISBN 978-0-9555930-1-7

Printed and designed: saltmedia.co.uk

Written and illustrated: Hugo Woolley.

Contents

Nothing appals me more than discussing business over breakfast, it can't be good for you, but Brunch is slightly different.

I believe this is an American invention for a meal as the name would imply, to be eaten in-between or instead of breakfast and lunch. This is a feast, usually informal – pyjamas and dressing gowns can be worn, at leisure, on Sundays with the papers and/or on holiday. It is more substantial than an early morning breakfast (well, mine are) and may go to two or three courses! Starter – main course – toast and jam or a 'puddingy' thing. These days, it is quite fashionable to have 'Brunch Meetings' in the City offices where the moguls of business can wheel and deal without the inconvenience of getting up early to slot in a hurried breakfast. Nothing appals me more than discussing business over breakfast, it can't be good for you, but Brunch is slightly different.

The Brunch dishes in this book are slightly more adventurous than breakfast dishes, possibly more substantial and are eaten over a period of up to four hours – you do not rush a Brunch! It should be regarded as more of a party meal. Talking at Brunch is more permissible than at Breakfast. But, you should gauge the mood of the other 'Brunchers' before launching into a diatribe about your 'goings on' of the previous evening or your latest holiday adventures!

Some of these recipes I enjoy, not only for Brunch but also for supper. I have included some snacks that are traditionally eaten in the very early hours; Breakfast eaten before you go to bed (if you go to bed at all!), after the last waltz has been played and you are beginning to sober up. These are more 'snacky' and could be called a 'Latefast'.

I have found that readers of 'Breakfast' – the previous book to this - wanted some idea of the most useful equipment to have at hand for Breakfast and Brunch cooking: Apart from the obvious frying pans, spatulas, wooden spoons and non-stick saucepans etc; I find Chefs' Rings invaluable – they come in 2 sizes but I find the smaller, 2 ¾ inch wide by 1 ½ inch deep (7cm x 3.5cm) ring the most useful, for shaping Fishcakes or Bubble and Squeak etc. I like good tools like a pallet knife and metal spatulas with quite sharp ends so that it is easy to slip under the most delicate of eggs or Porridge Brûlées (page 11). If you can't find Chef's Rings, a food tin-can, open at both ends would suffice. A food processor is essential, as is a hand whisk; these help with bread kneading and sauce whisking, all the

Brunch:

A more sophisticated breakfast.

things that require a lot of elbow grease. I have a gammy right arm, so these are important pieces of equipment. Even if you don't have a gammy arm – these useful items will stop you getting one!

I cook on a four-oven Aga and you will find most of the Brunches that require baking use only a couple of temperatures – 190°C or 230°C (bottom-right or top-right Aga oven). Fan-ovens cook a little warmer and you will have to reduce the temperatures by at least 20°C.

The poor old French and other Europeans have, in my experience, a terrible attitude to breakfast and Brunch – they are small, unimaginative breakfasts with lots of fluffy pastry. No wonder they are all so thin and take 3 hours over lunch! Breakfast and Brunch can be much maligned in the UK, not really taken seriously by some people, the same-old-things always turn up in the morning, dripping in fat or oil and made with second-rate produce. Take this meal seriously and you could survive through to dinner, feeling good and alert. This is, after all, a meal you can eat any time of day – unlike lunch or dinner or tea – who has ever heard of an 'all day lunch'?

The great joy of writing this book is the development of the recipes both traditional and innovative. Unfortunately, I always make a terrible mess and it is my wife, Pippa, who is the one that always seems to end up cleaning me and the kitchen, whilst I am setting up the photo, writing the recipes or going on to a new dish. It is mainly thanks to her patience 'Brunch' comes to you! This book, I hope will inspire you to an adventurous Brunch – you are not in as much of a hurry as you are for breakfast, so, impress a loved one, or an important guest or an in-law or two. You will get an immense amount of satisfaction and Brownie Points!

I am steadily trying to put together a list of like-minded places to have a good Breakfast or Brunch. If you have a favourite place for breakfast or Brunch, contact me through the website; **www.breakfastbook.co.uk**

(V) = vegetarian. (GF) = gluten free. (DF) = dairy free.

Who has ever heard of an 'all day lunch'?

Granola

(V, DF)

Similar to baked Muesli but with more in the way of nuts and seeds.

For a large bowl-full to keep one person going for a week:

2 tablespoons vegetable oil or clarified butter.

125ml (5 fl.oz.) warm water

3 tablespoons honey

3 tablespoons golden syrup.

1 teaspoon vanilla extract

A pinch of salt

300g (12oz.) Jumbo oats – porridge oats won't do for this recipe.

100g. (4 oz.) each: flaked almonds, desiccated coconut, sunflower seeds, pumpkin seeds, sesame seeds, and chopped pecan or walnuts.

1 teaspoon ground cinnamon.

100g (4 oz.) each: chopped dried apricots or sweetened dried cranberries and large Australian golden sultanas or any plump dried fruit.

The grated zest of ½ an orange.

Granola has its origins in America with the influences from North European immigrants. Similar to baked Muesli but with more in the way of nuts and seeds and sweetened with honey and/or Maple syrup and golden syrup. This recipe is not too sweet – some granola; mainly the proprietary brands, are so sweet, it is positively sickly (for us over 40 that is).

Heat the oven to: 230°C; 450°F; gas mark 8.

Mix the oil, warm water, honey, syrup, and vanilla essence together in a jug until the honey and syrup melts in with the water. In a large mixing bowl, mix the oats, almonds, coconut, seeds, nuts, and ground cinnamon and mix everything well. Pour over the sweetening mixture and mix together. When everything is thoroughly coated and slightly moistened (hate that word), tip it all out onto a large baking sheet or two baking sheets so that there is a thin layer of Granola on the sheet. Bake in the centre of the hot oven for 5 minutes, if you have two trays, put one in the centre and one on the top shelf of the oven, after 5 minutes, take out the trays, give them a mix so that all the Granola is toasted, then, put the trays back, swapping them from top to centre so that they get an equal toasting for another five minutes. Mix the granola and place the trays in the oven for a further 10 to 15 minutes, mixing every 5 minutes until the Granola is toasted a gold-brown and dry.

Remove from the oven and pour the Granola into a dry, big mixing bowl and mix in the dried fruit and orange zest. Allow to cool. When the Granola is cool, put into an air-tight container. You can store the Granola like this for 2 or 3 weeks.

If you like things even sweeter add 4 to 6 tablespoons maple syrup and use a little less water. Serve with a little milk or apple and/or orange juice, or a couple tablespoons low-fat yoghurt or sprinkle over fruit salad. Granola is very good for you; it has the same nutritional value as those awful cereals that you are made to eat if you are on a high fibre diet that taste like a cross between wet cardboard and sawdust!

Marmalade Bars:

(V)

One of our B&B guests suggested Ginger Marmalade or Lime Marmalade instead of ordinary Marmalade...

It's nice to have a snack to get you going in the morning. If you are one of these strange people who can only face a cup of coffee in the morning, these are very good for you to nibble. These bars are oaty, soft, but crunchy – they are a cross between a flapjack and cake and have a little tang from the marmalade. You could survive with just a Marmalade Bar in the morning. This is so simple; you could get the children to make them for you.

Preheat oven to 190°C; 375°F; Gas mark 5.

You need a non-stick baking pan – 32cm L x 18cm W x 3cm D (12 3/4ins L x 7 1/4ins w x 1 1/4ins D)

Melt the butter in a large mixing bowl in the microwave, add the sugar. Mix in the flour and the porridge oats so that the butter and sugar covers everything and the whole lot is thoroughly mixed in.

Spoon out half the mixture into the baking pan and flatten equally over the bottom using a pallet knife. Press down the mixture, into the corners, check it is the same thickness. Now spread the marmalade over the mixture, evenly distributing the shreds. Sprinkle on the sultanas and shredded apricots. Mix in the almonds into the rest of the oats, sugar and butter and spread the mixture over the top of the marmalade and flatten out as before. Heat up some honey in the microwave so it is very liquid, brush it or drizzle it on the top of the oat mixture, it will give the bars a shine.

Place in the middle shelf of the oven and bake for 30 to 35 minutes. When it is baked, allow it to cool in the baking tray. The mixture will firm up as it cools, ready for cutting into bars or squares.

These bars will keep for a week in an air-tight container. One of our B&B guests suggested Ginger Marmalade or Lime Marmalade instead of ordinary Marmalade which I thought a great idea (unfortunately, I hate both Ginger and Lime!).

For 12 large or 24 small bars:

250g (9oz.) butter.

200g (7oz.) light soft brown, sugar.

150g (5oz.) self-raising flour

350g (12oz.) porridge oats

3 or 4 tablespoons of your favourite marmalade – it should have thin-cut shreds and be tangy.

50g (2oz.) sultanas

50g (2oz.) ready-to-eat, dried apricots sliced thinly, like marmalade shreds.

50g (2oz.) sliced Almonds.

About **2 tablespoons** honey.

Rice Porridge
(GF, V)

A cold rice pudding breakfast, very popular in Asia and India.

For 4 to 6 people:

100g (4oz.) flaked pudding rice or ordinary pudding rice – note the simmering times on the packet might be different.

400ml (1 can) coconut milk.

400ml - a can full of semi-skimmed ordinary milk

Pinch nutmeg – a couple of scrapes from a whole nutmeg.

2 tablespoons runny honey.

An inch knob of fresh ginger, peeled and finely grated.

A ripe mango.

50g (2oz.) flaked almonds, toasted in a hot oven for 5 minutes.

A drizzle of honey.

Some Rice Porridge is savoury and some is just rice and water boiled up for ages producing a very unappetising porridge – but very good glue! This is a Thai adaptation.

Put the rice, milk, coconut milk and nutmeg into a pan and bring slowly to a simmer, stirring all the time. Simmer for 8 minutes, stirring quite regularly, allowing the mixture to thicken. If you can't find flaked pudding rice and are using ordinary pudding rice, you will need to simmer for about 25 minutes. If it thickens too much and the rice is still hard, reduce the heat, add a little water or milk and continue stirring until it becomes a thick sauce.

Meanwhile, peel off the skin of a mango, cut in half, running the knife down the flat, round stone in the middle. Cut the flesh into little cubes. (You can do this without peeling but I find it impossible to describe! They do it a lot on television cooking shows, so, watch out for it.) Toast the almonds for about 5 minutes in a hot oven.

Add the honey and the ginger to the porridge stir a few times, taste to see if it is sweet enough for you then remove from the heat, pour into a shallow bowl and allow to cool. Serve warm or cold – nicer, in my view, cold.

Spoon out two or three tablespoons of porridge into a little bowl to serve, add a spoon of mango chunks and almonds. Drizzle some more honey over the top. For different topping; squish out some pomegranate seeds out of a halved pomegranate and some skinned pistachio nuts and sprinkle them over the top of the porridge or; fresh blueberries, roasted crushed pecan nuts and maple syrup (very American).

Porridge Brûlée
and Prune Compote
(V)

I love this light, slightly stylish, Brunch starter. Who would have thought that such humble ingredients – eggs, prunes, cream, porridge oats – could produce such a wonderful Brunch! It is best prepared the day before and finished off and served the next morning/ early afternoon. This is usually our Christmas morning treat.

Put the prunes, orange slices and the cinnamon stick into a saucepan and fill with water to just below the surface of the fruit. Bring slowly to the boil; reduce to a simmer for five minutes. Remove from the heat and pour in the apple juice, stir and leave to cool overnight. In the morning, take out the cinnamon stick and serve the compote cold.

Put the egg yolks, caster sugar (and vanilla essence, if required) into a large glass mixing bowl. With an electric whisk (or a balloon whisk, if you have the muscles) whisk the eggs and sugar until they turn pale. Gradually add the hot milk, constantly whisking and then pour in the cream and the porridge oats, whisk gently for another 30 seconds and then cover and place in the fridge for at least 8 hours or over-night.

Pre-heat the oven 130°C; 250°F; Gas Mark 1.

Seal one end of 8 Chefs' Rings (3½ cm deep x 7cm wide rings, or 2¾ ins x 1½ ins wide) with a couple of layers of cling-film to form a cup. Place the cups onto a baking tray. Whisk up the Brûlée mixture, to separate the porridge, and equally pour into the rings. Place into the oven and bake for 45 minutes. Remove from the oven and allow the Brûlées to cool.

To serve; gently remove the cling-film; place the ring onto the centre of a plate, gently peal the cling-film off the bottom of the chef-ring, not lifting the ring too high off the plate – like removing a sticking plaster off a particularly sore wound. Sprinkle some Golden caster sugar over the top; run a clean, small knife around the inside of the ring and gently raise the ring, leaving the Brûlée behind. With a mini-blowtorch, melt the sugar on top. Put a tablespoon of cold compote on the side and serve with pride. You will find the porridge forms a little base to the light custard on top. The thin, crispy layer of sugar just needs a little tap to break into that creamy wonderfulness – I am getting carried away.

If you can't find Chefs' Rings, use ramekins, unfortunately, you will not be able to turn the Brûlées out. I find Chefs' Rings invaluable and use them for a lot of things; from forming fishcakes and potato hash cakes, to help presenting food on the plate.

To serve 8 (or 4 Trenchermen).

For Prune Compote:

250g (9oz) pitted prunes,

½ small orange, quartered and very thinly sliced.

A cinnamon stick.

½ litre (17fl.oz.) apple juice – preferably the cloudy type .

For the Porridge Brûlée:

5 egg yolks (use the whites for Egg White Omelette Page 30)

50g (2oz.) caster vanilla sugar – sugar that has had a vanilla pod resting in it for ages

– or:

A teaspoon vanilla essence - if you don't have vanilla sugar.

100ml (4fl.oz.) hot full fat milk.

475ml (16fl.oz.) double cream or (whipping cream if you prefer a light Brûlée).

35g (1½ oz.) porridge oats.

100g (4 oz.) golden caster sugar or Demerara sugar.

Coffee
Compote Crumble
(GF, V):

For the Compote:

A total weight of **250g (8oz) of**:

Ready-to-eat dried apricots, Dried figs (halved), Pitted prunes, Dried apple rings (halved), 'Golden' or Australian sultanas, Raisins.

Half a lemon, halved and very thinly sliced.

1 cinnamon stick.

Half litre (18 fl.oz.) apple juice – preferably the cloudy type.

For topping:

50g (2oz) Demerara sugar – the more unrefined, the better.

50g (2oz) Plain white flour.

Half a teaspoon ground cinnamon.

1 teaspoon zest of lemon.

50g (2oz) Rolled or Jumbo oats (or porridge oats).

40g (1½ oz.) very cold butter.

500ml (just under a pint) thick Yoghurt full-fat or low fat.

2 tablespoons of cooled, strong espresso coffee.

We enjoy this in the winter months, don't know why, it just seems a more 'wintery' thing; it is a comforting something to start with.

We enjoy this in the winter months, don't know why, it just seems a more 'wintery' thing; it is a comforting something to start with.

You will need four 200ml (half pint) cappuccino cups. If you think the cups will be too much, you can do this using 8 large ramekins. I have used glasses for you to see the layers.

Pre-heat the oven - 200°C; 400°F; gas mark 6.

Put all the fruit and the cinnamon stick into a saucepan and fill with water to just below the surface of the fruit. Bring slowly to the boil; reduce to a simmer for 10 minutes. Remove from the heat and pour in the apple juice to just above the surface of the fruit, stir in and leave to cool overnight.

Put into the food processor with pastry blades – the sugar, flour, oats, cinnamon, lemon zest and the butter in small cubes. Give the mixture 2 second bursts, two or three times with the 'pulse' button. If you do not use a food processor, rub the same ingredients, with your finger-tips, in a bowl until the crumble resembles big bread crumbs. Spread the crumble thinly on a thick baking sheet and place in the pre-heated oven for 5 minutes. Remove from the oven and mix the crumble up, spread out evenly again and put back in the oven for another five minutes. Remove and leave to cool. If the crumble is not crumbly enough, pop the tray back in for a couple more minutes.

Mix the yoghurt with the coffee. Divide the fruit compote between the cappuccino coffee cups. Pour in the yoghurt equally leaving at least 2cm (0.75 ins) gap to the top. Sprinkle the crumble over the top of each. Pat down gently and put into the fridge for at least an hour. The juice of the fruit will mingle with the yoghurt.

Salad with Fruit

(V,DF,GF)

Pippa – my wife – thinks that people should have lots of fruit in the morning, but, there is nothing more boring than a fruit-bowl full of 'raw fruit'. Here are some more interesting alternatives:

As opposed to Fruit Salad; this salad has an unusual sharp dressing – a real eye-opener. All the fruit have some kind of medicinal property in them, things like anti-carcinogens, stuff that lowers cholesterol, anti oxidants, also lots of vitamins and fibre:

Whisk all these ingredients together and taste to see if you would prefer it sweeter or sharper. I have also added a couple of grinds of black pepper – believe it or not – this brings out a lot of the sweet flavours. You could add any other fruit like strawberries or Star fruit, but, I would not use oranges or grapefruit unless you compensate the sharpness with the dressing. I would avoid bananas, Kiwi fruit etc; soft fruits – they go into mush nearly instantly.

Serve with a little fat-free crème fraiche or yoghurt – it is, however, best and better for you on its own. One feels particularly virtuous after a bowl of this salad.

For a generous bowl for 2 people:

For the Fruit:

1 mango, slice off the flesh from the huge central stone, cut into slices and cut off the skin. Chop into chunks in to a large mixing bowl.

1 pomegranate, cut in half and squeeze out the juicy pips, or remove them with a little spoon. A ripe pomegranate will be quite juicy so, try and cut it in half over the fruit mixing bowl, without slicing your hand! Remove any white pith that might escape into the bowl when you scrape out the pips.

2 thick slices of fresh pineapple. Slice off the skin and the centre core and chop into chunks. Add to the mixing bowl.

3 tablespoons of fresh Blueberries.

A quarter of a water melon, chopped into chunks - try to remove as many pips as possible – or keep them in, they are quite good for your digestion.

For the Salad Dressing whisk together, in a small bowl:

2 tablespoons runny honey or maple syrup (which is not as sweet as honey).

2 tablespoons lemon juice.

3 tablespoons cranberry juice.

2 tablespoons Raspberry (or strawberry or red wine) vinegar.

Or **1 tablespoon** of Balsamic vinegar if you cannot find the former.

Orange Salad

(V,GF,DF)

If you want to
serve this as a refreshing
intercourse dish at a
dinner party, add some
Kirsch or orange liquor.

Oh, what joy! This is not only my favourite fruity-thing in the morning, but possibly the simplest thing to make. It is so simple, I debated whether to include it in this sophisticated recipe book. I decided it is a vital late summer part of breakfast and Brunch and should be in these pages.

Cut the skin off 2 ordinary and 2 blood oranges or a grapefruit. The art is to run the knife just under the white pith and not take too much of the flesh. A very sharp knife is always good for this job. Don't throw the skins of 2 of the oranges.

In **250ml (just over ½ pt)** water, put in **half** a cinnamon stick and **2 tablespoons** Demerara sugar (Demerara sugar has a little more character and brings out the orange flavours), **a small sprig (about 5 cm – 2 ins)** fresh rosemary. Put all these ingredients in a saucepan with the orange peel of 2 of the oranges. Bring the water to the boil and simmer for 5 minutes. Then, allow to cool with the bits in – strain off the bits when the liquid is cool.

Slice the oranges as thinly as possible. Slice them from side to side; not stem to stern, if you see what I mean. This shows off the segments of the orange. Be very careful; for some reason the only time I cut myself - in 35 years of 'cheffing' - is when I slice oranges!! Place the slices neatly in a bowl and pour over the liquor. And that's it – that simple, but very, very popular for Brunch.

If you want to serve this as a refreshing intercourse dish at a dinner party, add some Kirsch or orange liquor.

Poached Pears
and Jelly
(V)

Adrian serves this in his restaurant for pudding, which I never have room for. I take it home and have mine for breakfast which is far more enjoyable!

An Autumn treat. Make the day before. My friend Adrian - chef/ proprietor at the famous Padstow Restaurant, Margot's Bistro - helped me with this; he adds saffron to his Poached Pears – a little different and very stylish! Adrian serves this in his restaurant for pudding, which I never have room for. I take it home and have mine for breakfast which is far more enjoyable!

Peel the pears leaving the stalks on. Place the pears, the half lemon in a saucepan with a lid. Put in enough water to cover the fruit. Add the rest of the ingredients (not the gelatine). Put on a lid, bring to the boil and then reduce the heat to a simmer for 30 minutes – or when the fruit is soft. This will depend as to how big the pears are and how ripe. Test by putting in a small knife and if the knife slides out with ease, they are ready.

Gently remove the pears and set aside to cool. Try to stand them on their bottoms. Take out the lemon and squeeze out any juice into the liquor. Bring the liquor up to a simmer and reduce by about a third – about 30 minutes. Then stir 4 sheets of gelatine soaked in water until it becomes rubbery (Discard the water) into 500ml (17 fl.oz.) of the hot liquor. When the gelatine has melted pour the liquid into 4 or 6 small, metal pie moulds about 8cm x 5cm high and, when the liquid has cooled, put the pears and the jelly into the fridge.

To serve; pop the jelly moulds into some hot water for a couple of secs, to loosen the jelly, turn onto a plate, then slice a thin slice off the bottom of the pear to allow it to stand on a plate safely. Serve with some thick yoghurt or crème fraiche or (if in Cornwall) some clotted cream, or simply on its own.

For 4 to 6 people:
6 large or 8 small pears:
350g (12oz.) caster sugar.
½ a lemon.
Pinch of saffron.
2 medium size fresh bay leaves.
250ml (9fl.oz.) dry, full white wine.
4 sheets gelatine.

Grapefruit Granita
(V,GF,DF)

For extra sweetness; pour some Cassis over the top of the Granita
– it produces wonderful colours as well!

For 4 people or a tub to yourself!

25g (1oz.) granulated sugar.

600 ml (1 pint) water.

300 ml (½ pint) fresh grapefruit juice – about 3 grapefruits. If you can get a bit of the pulp from the squeezer (about a tablespoon) it will give the Granita some texture. Try to use the fresh as carton does not make a very good Granita.

2 teaspoons of grated grapefruit rind.

A very refreshing water-ice for the morning. This will wake you up and inject some vitamins. Serve with a Shrewsbury Biscuit (page 17) or a Madeleine from the 'Breakfast' book (page 15).

Melt the sugar in the water in a saucepan, stir over a moderate heat until the sugar has dissolved, then bring to the boil and boil for 5 minutes.

Cool to room temperature and add the fruit juice and stir in the zest, place onto a large, wide plastic freezer-proof tray and put into the freezer until it has turned to a soft icy, snowy texture. Stir up the crystals and put back into the freezer. Then stir up the Granita again after 30 minutes. Repeat this process a couple more times until you have a smooth, sorbet consistency. If it freezes solid, allow it to melt for half an hour out in the kitchen or two hours in the fridge and then stir it up again to the desired texture.

Serve in a Sundae Glass with Shrewsbury Biscuits (page 17). I enjoy putting in a straw so that you can suck up the juice as it melts. For extra sweetness; pour some Cassis over the top of the Granita – it produces wonderful colours as well!

Shrewsbury Biscuit
(V)

If you enjoy the slightly aniseed, scented taste of caraway seeds, add a tablespoon to the dough.

This is a very old fashioned biscuit. It is sweet, and a hint of savoury if you add caraway seeds and Rose Water which is how they are traditionally made. It compliments the sourness of grapefruit wonderfully. Serve it with Grapefruit Granita (page 16).

Preheat oven 190° C; 375° F; gas mark 5.

Cream the butter and the sugar with a hand-whisk until pale. Gradually whisk in the egg and the rose water. Sift in the flour and baking powder and mix in with the rest of the ingredients, add the lemon zest. Mix into a fairly firm dough – add a little more flour if necessary. (Knead in the caraway seeds at this stage). Turn out the dough onto a floured surface and knead for about 2 minutes.

Roll the dough out to about 1½ cm (½ ins) thick and cut into fingers about 10cm. by 2cm. (4 x 1 ins) and lay them on a baking sheet lined with baking parchment, at least 2cm apart. Bake the biscuits for 15 minutes, until lightly browned and firm to the touch. The biscuits will grow bigger. Cut the biscuits and lay to cool on a cooling rack. Store in an airtight container or biscuit tin.

Traditionally, Shrewsbury Biscuits have caraway seeds as well, but I am not partial to them. If you enjoy the slightly aniseed, scented taste of caraway seeds, add a tablespoon to the dough.

For about 24 biscuits:

110g (4oz.) soft butter.

150g (5oz.) caster sugar.

1 large egg.

2 teaspoons rose water.

225g (8oz.) plain flour.

1 teaspoon baking powder.

The zest of **one** lemon.

(**A tablespoon** of caraway seeds – optional)

Cinnamon Hotcakes

(V)

A great accompaniment with anything including blueberries and ice cream, sliced bananas and maple syrup, crispy bacon and scrambled eggs.

For about 20 hotcakes:

200g (7oz.) self-raising flour.

1 teaspoon ground cinnamon.

1 teaspoon baking powder.

½ teaspoon Bicarbonate of Soda.

2 large eggs.

200ml (7fl.oz.) low-fat yoghurt.

100ml (4fl.oz.) milk.

2 tablespoons maple syrup.

Oil for frying.

A cross between a pancake, a drop scone and a waffle. This is a great accompaniment with anything including blueberries and ice cream, sliced bananas and maple syrup, crispy bacon and scrambled eggs. Or on their own with butter and jam.

Sift the flour, cinnamon, baking powder and bicarbonate of soda into a mixing bowl. Into another mixing bowl, whisk all the liquid ingredients together – not the oil. With a hand-whisk running, pour the liquid into the centre of the flour and whisk the liquid ingredients into the flour, drawing the flour into the centre and ensuring the whole lot forms a thick batter.

Heat a non-stick frying pan to quite a high heat. Put in a drop of oil and brush it around the pan. Put in a tablespoon of batter and cook until bubbles form on the top of the cake. Flip over and cook for about 30 to 45 seconds. Cook 2 or 3 hotcakes at a time. Serve as soon as possible. Keep the hotcakes – as their name would imply – warm and serve warm.

You could add fruit in with the batter such as; a couple of tablespoons of Blueberries, or some mashed up, ripe bananas or yellow Australian sultanas. The batter could be made the night before. But it could thicken up so, whisk in a tablespoon or two of milk before cooking.

Beetroot Pancakes (V)

Sweet Potato Pancake (V)

This and the sweet potato pancake don't taste like they sound (if you know what I mean). They go with both sweet and savoury dishes or can be served on their own.

To make 14 to 16 pancakes.

250g (9oz.) cooked fresh beetroot, peeled and cooled.

3 tablespoons crème fraiche.

4 eggs.

1 tablespoon caster sugar.

A good pinch (1/2 teaspoon) cinnamon.

100g (4oz.) self raising flour.

1 teaspoon baking powder.

Tablespoon melted butter.

Vegetable or groundnut oil for frying.

To make 14 to 16 pancakes.

250g (9oz.) peeled, sweet potato, chopped into small chunks, cooked for about 15 minutes and cooled.

3 tablespoons crème fraiche.

4 eggs.

1 tablespoon caster sugar.

½ teaspoon vanilla essence.

75g (3oz.) self raising flour.

1 teaspoon baking powder.

Tablespoon melted butter.

Vegetable or groundnut oil for frying.

An adapted recipe of an 18th Century, colourful pancake. It was said to be best eaten with game – something eaten regularly for breakfast in the 'old days'. This and the sweet potato pancake don't taste like they sound (if you know what I mean). They go with both sweet and savoury dishes or can be served on their own.

Whiz up the lot (not the oil for frying) in a food processor into a batter. Allow the mixture to rest for 30 minutes and then heat a little oil and put a tablespoon of the mixture into the pan. Turn after bubbles form on the top (they cook and burn quite quickly) and serve in a 'stack' warm or cold, with sweet or savoury dishes.

Something I thought would go well with the Beetroot Pancake – again sweetish, not savoury and a lovely looking pancake.

Whiz up the lot (not the oil for frying) in a food processor into a batter. Allow the mixture to rest for 30 minutes and then heat a little oil and put a tablespoon of the mixture into the pan. Turn after bubbles form on the top and serve in a 'stack' – warm. Try with a dollop of crème fraiche or clotted cream and with raspberry or strawberry sauce or coulis.

Baking Brioche

(V)

...for the authentic French way; just dip toasted Brioche in a bowl of black coffee. You will then feel very Parisian and thin!

For 1 loaf:

12g (½ oz.) fresh yeast. I have tried and constantly failed with dried, baking yeast and it appears the real thing is best! If all you have is dried yeast, follow the instructions on the packet implicitly.

1 tablespoon caster sugar.

100ml (4 fl.oz.) tepid milk.

225g (8oz.) strong white flour.

½ teaspoon salt.

100g (4oz.) unsalted butter.

2 large eggs.

Cream the sugar and the yeast in a small mixing bowl. Use your warm fingers or a wooden spoon. Stir in the slightly warm, blood temperature milk and put to one side to allow the yeast to grow. Meanwhile, sieve the flour and salt into a food processor with the pastry blades installed. With the machine running, add the butter gradually in lumps and then the yeast mixture and the eggs. Mix to a soft dough, and continue to knead for at least a minute. Cover the bowl with oiled cling-film (so that the dough does not stick to it) and leave to 'prove' for at least an hour in a warm place. The dough should double in size.

Pre-heat the oven 190°C; 375°F or Gas mark 5 (Aga bottom right).

When the dough has proved, 'knock back' or knead the dough again in the processor for another minute and then scrape out the dough into a buttered 450g. (1 lb.) loaf tin or a Brioche mould (a tin that looks like a giant fairy cake tin). Lightly dust the top of the dough with some flour and cover with a clean cloth, prove again for at least an hour. When it has proved, take off the cloth, gently place into the oven and bake for 35 to 40 minutes, cover the top with foil if it starts to turn too brown. Turn out on to a wire rack once baked and allow to cool.

Serve toasted Brioche with a Saucisse de Corbet (page 40) and some fried streaky bacon or Pancetta and an egg of your choice for a very continental Brunch or slice up some French sausages and make a sandwich with lots of Dijon Mustard (a Provencal Brunch). Or for the authentic French way; just dip toasted Brioche in a bowl of black coffee. You will then feel very Parisian and thin!

Brioche is a buttery bread the French enjoy, especially for breakfast. It is a difficult bread to make – nothing like as easy as ordinary bread! The dough is quite 'wet' and very difficult to handle – have a go. I once bought brioche from a supermarket and it was totally wrong – it was more like a cake; sweet, inedible and riddled with vanilla for some reason – tasted like solid, floury custard! If you live in the middle of the country, far away from the sophisticated metropolis, like we do, this is the only way you will obtain this wonderful, light breakfast bread.

Brioche French Toast
and Pear

(V)

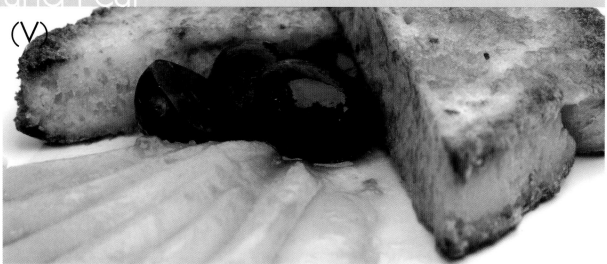

My son suggested a dusting of icing sugar but I would find that too sweet – entirely up to you – and if you are young enough.

A French Brunch that is more substantial than most French Breakfasts or Brunches. I now understand why all the French – well, the Parisians – are so thin. They don't eat anything substantial until supper, they only have a cigarette and black coffee when they get up in the morning!

Beat the egg with the milk in a flat dish. Lightly toast the Brioche slice then soak both sides in the egg, ensure you soak up as much egg as possible. Melt half the butter in a clean frying pan over a medium heat. Add a teaspoon of oil to stop the butter burning. Fry the soaked slice – be careful, the Brioche is quite fragile and will probably need a spatula to ease it into the pan. Fry for a couple of minutes on each side. Cut the slice in half and fry the cut sides for another 30 seconds or until slightly coloured. Put the slice onto a hot plate, keep warm.

Remove the stalk and the core from the peeled pear and slice the pear into about 6 slices (depending how big the pear is), try not to cut all the way through at the stalk end – this will help to keep the 'fan' together. Fan out the slices. Melt the rest of the butter in the same frying pan, add the sugar. When the sugar has melted with the butter, bring up the heat and add the lemon juice, then the brandy and allow it to boil for a minute – you could set fire to it (Flambé – that is) – that will help get rid of the alcohol. Reduce the heat and gently put the pear-fan into the mixture and cook for about 30 seconds. After that, baste the sauce over the pear to cook the top a little. With a palette knife or good spatula, lift the pear out and place onto the plate with the Eggy Brioche. Spoon over some sauce over the pear, garnish with some grapes cut in half and serve.

My son suggested a dusting of icing sugar but I would find that too sweet – entirely up to you – and if you are young enough.

Per substantial Frenchman:

A thick slice of Brioche, about 1½ cm. (½ ins) thick.

1 large egg.

A teaspoon milk.

A pear, peeled and cut in half.

1 tablespoon unsalted butter.

1 tablespoon soft brown sugar.

Juice of a quarter of a lemon.

1 tablespoon Cognac.

Autumn Pear
& Brioche Casserole

(V)

For a Christmassy touch; use mincemeat and apples instead of pears as the pears delicate flavours might be overwhelmed. This dish makes a good pudding with apricot jam instead of marmalade.

For six to 8 people.

3 pears, peeled, cut into quarters and cored.

About **half a pint of water (300ml).**

75g (3oz.) Demerara sugar.

The juice of **1** lemon and a couple of strips of the rind.

568ml (1 pint) double cream.

1 litre (1¾ pts) milk.

1 vanilla pod, split in half.

5 eggs

6 egg yolks (use the whites for Egg White Omelette (page 30)

140g (5oz.) caster sugar.

1 Brioche loaf (page 20) cut into 2cm. (1 ins) slices to produce about 8 slices excluding the end crusts.

About **50g (2oz.)** softened butter, plus extra for greasing.

Half a jar of your favourite marmalade, you may need to chop up the larger lumps of peel.

2 more tablespoons Demerara sugar.

This is a typical American-style breakfast or brunch, nice for Autumn and Christmas, sweet and wholesome, and no compromise for cholesterol! You could prepare this the night before. I wish I had the imagination to call it something else – other than 'Casserole' – it conjures up a stew or a savoury hotpot in my mind. It could be a kind of 'Autumn Bread and Butter Pudding with Marmalade, Brioche and Pears' – but that's too long winded. There is a savoury American Breakfast Casserole on page 38.

Put the pears into a large saucepan – the bigger the better. Cover with the water and Demerara sugar and bring to the boil. Add the lemon rind and juice and bring to a simmer. Poach for 15 minutes – or until the pears are tender. Drain the pears and leave to cool –use the poaching water for fruit salad (except it can be a bit too sweet).

Heat up the cream and the milk, with the split vanilla pod – not quite to the boil. Remove from the heat and allow the vanilla pod to infuse for half an hour. With a hand whisk, beat the eggs and the caster sugar until they turn pale. Scrape out the vanilla pod seeds into the milk – throw away the pod after removing the seeds, and then, with the whisk still running, slowly pour in the warm creamy milk to make a sort of custard.

Butter a pudding baking dish (about 20cm x 30cm – 8ins x 12 ins). Now, butter each slice of Brioche and cut in half, lengthways. Spread each slice with some marmalade, layer the base of the dish with some slices of brioche, marmalade-side up. Slice the pears thinly and lay them on top of the brioche. Pour over a third of the custard mixture and repeat the layers, with a layer of brioche on the top, marmalade side up and the pears neatly arranged. Pour over what is left of the custard mix. Leave in the fridge for 10 to 15 minutes to soak and absorb the liquid.

Pre-heat the oven 190°C; 375°F or Gas mark 5 (Aga bottom right).

Sprinkle the surface of the casserole with some golden caster sugar and bake for 40 minutes. Leave to cool for about 20 to 30 minutes (whilst you have your bacon and eggs or something more adventurous) and serve slightly warm.

Hawaiian Breakfast

(V)

...just as enjoyable in a flat in Clapham in February!

Think of a wonderful tropical beach, a dusky maiden (or hunk) with a huge smile and this exotic breakfast, she/he serves you at a table at the waters edge with little waves lapping at your toes – what a wonderful morning. A Brunch just as enjoyable in a flat in Clapham in February! This is not particularly fattening if you use low fat crème fraiche and is also a very good way of getting fruit into fussy children in the morning!

In a flat bottomed pudding bowl break in the eggs and beat lightly with a dash of milk. Soak the cut side of the croissants in the beaten egg (or each side of the bread with the mixture, try to give each slice an equal soaking). Put the pineapple, grapes and coconut into a mixing bowl, mix in the almonds, honey and finally crème fraiche. The crème fraiche will loosen up with the juice from the fruit.

Melt the butter with a touch of oil to stop it burning, in a clean frying pan, over a medium heat. Slide the croissants soaked in egg into the frying pan, eggy side of the croissants down, fry until golden brown. Put the croissants onto plates – eggy side up. Place the pineapple mixture in the centre of the croissants (or eggy bread). Serve immediately with a sprinkle of blueberries or redcurrants to decorate.

For 2 people:

2 croissants cut in half **or 2 thick slices** of white bread.

2 large eggs.

A dash of milk.

1 slice of fresh pineapple, the core removed and chopped

About **a dozen** green grapes (preferably seedless) sliced in half.

2 tablespoons sliced toasted almonds.

3 tablespoons crème fraiche

1 tablespoon runny honey.

2 tablespoons desiccated coconut.

A knob of unsalted butter and a dash of oil.

A few fresh blueberries or redcurrants.

Banana Bread

(V)

You will – I can assure you – be making tons of this bread!

For about a pound loaf:

Pre-heat oven 190°C; 375°F; Gas Mk. 5.

In a food processor with the double blades or the plastic dough blades put in:

3 large or 4 small bananas

75g (3oz.) soft butter.

200g (8oz.) granulated sugar.

1 large egg.

1 teaspoon vanilla essence.

1 teaspoon baking soda.

A pinch of salt.

Whiz these together with the 'pulse' button on the food processor so it is nicely mixed then add;

200g (8oz.) plain flour.

Just the best way to use up old bananas. I also found that my local big supermarket was flogging off over-ripe bananas cheaply. You will – I can assure you – be making tons of this bread! It is more of a cake than bread as it is not made with yeast. Very good on picnics. I like to do this in a food processor, but if you like a lumpy, rustic effect, use a large bowl and a wooden spoon to mix everything up with a lot of elbow power.

Mix all the ingredients together in the processor until you have a smooth batter. Butter a 10cm x 20cm (5 x 8 ins) loaf tin, cut out some baking parchment to fit the bottom of the tin and pour in the batter mix. Put in the centre of the oven and bake for 60 minutes. Check after 45 minutes to see if the top is brown enough, if it is, finish off the baking with some foil to stop the top burning.

Nectarine
Danish Pastry

(V)

To make 6 pastries.

375g pack of puff pastry, preferable ready rolled.

3 to 4 ripe nectarines, depending on size.

25g (1 oz.) butter.

Juice of half a lemon.

55g (2oz.) Demerara sugar.

1 teaspoon vanilla extract.

2 teaspoons cornflour mixed with **2 tablespoons** cold water.

25g (1oz.) melted butter.

For the frosting:

4 tablespoons icing sugar.

1 teaspoon lemon juice.

Water.

These freeze well un-cooked or baked, so you can make a whole batch and produce them when you want.

This is for those Europeans who have very small, fluffy-pastry-type breakfasts and brunch. These freeze well un-cooked or baked, so you can make a whole batch and produce them when you want. You can have them with or without frosting (best with, in my view). I like to dollop the frosting on with a spoon so it looks home made. I like everybody to see that I haven't gone out to the local supermarket and picked up the usual Danish pastry. Anyway; what supermarket or baker is going to serve Nectarine Danishes?!!

Roll out the pastry to ½ cm thick and 35cm x 22.5cm (13 ¾ x 9 ins). Then cut into 6 equal squares 12 x 12 cm (4 ¾ ins). Remember, if you need to re-roll the pastry again, just fold the bits together so that it keeps the puffy layers in the pastry – don't munge it all up like you would a dough or short-crust pastry. Keep the squares chilled in the fridge whilst you make the filling.

For the filling, halve then stone the nectarines. Slice each half into 6 to 8 slices. Melt the butter, lemon juice and sugar in a wide-based saucepan and allow the sugar to melt, stirring all the time over a gentle heat. Add the nectarines and the vanilla extract and toss gently in the butter and remove from the heat.

Pre-heat the oven to 230°C; 450°F; Gas mark 8.

Take each pastry square and place onto a baking sheet lined with baking parchment. Twist one corner one way a full twist, the opposite corner a full twist the other way. Lift out 6 or 8 slices of nectarine with a fork, leaving the juice in the pan, and arrange in a neat row from twisted corner to the other twisted corner. Fold the non-twisted corners over the top of the filling, pinch together and twist to seal. Repeat this with the other five pastries. Warm up the juice in the pan and stir in the cornflour and water mixture. This will thicken the sauce. When the sauce is nice and thick and cooked through, spoon a couple of teaspoons onto the exposed fruit on each pastry. When you have made all the pastries, put them into a fridge to cool for an hour.

Meanwhile, make the frosting. Just mix the ingredients together into a smooth paste. It should be nearly as thick as runny toothpaste. Add water or more sugar to get it to the right consistency. Keep at room temperature.

Bake the pastries for 15 to 20 minutes. When they are golden brown, take them out and place on a cooling rack. Brush each pastry with melted butter. Spoon the frosting over the Danishes whilst they are hot and serve when they have cooled a bit but are still warm. If you are adept enough; make a cone out of greaseproof paper, fill it with frosting, snip off the end and pipe the frosting in little lines over the top of the Danish. They won't, however, look very home made! Do this on a cooling rack (with a bit of paper underneath to catch the spills). If you are freezing the pastries, don't put on the frosting. You can bake the cooked ones from frozen: about **15 minutes at oven temp. 180°C; 350°F; Gas Mk. 4.**

Blinis are a little pancake from Russia made with buckwheat – a gluten free grain, related to rhubarb, not, as one supposes, to wheat. It is

Blinis for Brunch
(V,GF-with Buckwheat only)

It is best not to store blinis but to eat them the day you make them.

To make 12 to 15 Blinis:

150ml (¼ pt) warm milk.

½ teaspoon dried yeast
or **6g (¼ oz.)** fresh yeast.

1 teaspoon sugar.

175g (6oz.) plain four or, if you can find
it, buckwheat flour.

1 large egg.

Pinch of salt.

Oil for frying.

more of a bread than a pancake. In Russia, you would cover your Blinis with soured cream and Caviar (see page 27). You can serve blinis with tons of things for Brunch; smoked salmon and scrambled egg; cottage cheese and jam and many other things; there are a couple of other suggestions below.

Put the yeast into a bowl (crumble fresh yeast) and add the sugar, pour in the warm (body temperature) milk. Whisk the milk and the yeast to mix thoroughly and leave in a warm place for at least 10 minutes – until there are bubbles over the surface of the milk.

Sift in the flour into a mixing bowl with a pinch of salt. Whisk the egg into the milk and yeast. With a hand-whisk, beat in the milk mixture into the flour gradually, until a thick batter forms. Allow the batter to rest for 10 minutes. Heat a small amount of vegetable oil in a thick bottom pan or skillet, and spoon in one dessertspoon of the batter. If you find the batter is too thick after resting (sticks to the spoon - does not pour off the spoon), slacken it off by whisking in a little more milk – but not too much. Flatten out the batter a little and allow the batter to firm up and then flip over the Blinis and fry the other side. It will puff up into a bready-type, small pancake and ready to serve.

It is best not to store blinis but to eat them the day you make them. Shop-bought blinis have some sort of preservative in them that ensures they keep their rather unappetising rubberyness!

Blinis with Caviar,
served 'Polonaise':

What luxury; what decadence you should always serve Champagne or, for true authenticity; vodka served in a block of ice

2 hard-boiled eggs.

A tablespoon finely chopped parsley and capers.

4 Blinis - the flatter, the better (Page 26). You could use Scotch Pancakes or Drop Scones for these snacks except they may be a little too sweet.

4 teaspoons soured cream.

½ teaspoon cream of horseradish.

4 teaspoons Caviar (or lumpfish caviar, for economy).

Place 2 eggs in a saucepan of warm water, bring to the boil and boil for 8 minutes. Immediately, plunge the eggs in cold running water and leave the eggs in the cold water until they are cold. Prepare the eggs 'Polonaise' – an old fashioned accompaniment for Caviar: cut the eggs in half and remove the yolks. The yolks should not have any grey on them, if they have; they have been cooked too long or they are not very fresh. Finely chop up the yolks and the white, keep them separate. Arrange on a nice platter; the chopped egg yolk, then the chopped whites, the chopped parsley and capers and finally, a couple of teaspoons of Caviar. You could present then in four quarters of a circle.

Mix the horseradish with the soured cream and place in a little bowl. Put some crushed ice in a large bowl and put the plate with the Caviar Polonaise on top to keep cool. To serve the Caviar; there should be two silver teaspoons (or Mother of Pearl for pure elegance, as pictured). Keep everything cold; spoons, bowls and plates. Serve the Blinis whilst they are still warm. What luxury; what decadence; you should always serve Champagne or, for true authenticity; vodka served in a block of ice: If you have an old gallon ice cream tub; fill it with water (use filtered water as it will give you clear ice), stick half a cork onto the bottom of the vodka bottle, put the bottle into the centre of the tub (you might have to secure it with some string or sticky tape), pop it in the freezer so that the water freezes round the bottle – this will take a couple of days. Pop the block out of the ice cream tub just before serving.

Ham and Marmalade
Blinis

4 quite large Blinis (page 26).

Unsalted butter, slightly softened or olive oil-type low-fat spread.

4 teaspoons thick-cut traditional marmalade. Chop up the 'shreds' a bit, so it is not too lumpy.

50g (2oz.) good, sliced, smoked ham.

2 tablespoons crème fraiche or cream cheese.

Tablespoon chopped fresh sage.

Ground pepper.

Spread butter or low-fat spread on one side of 4 blinis. Take a pastry cutter that is the same size as the blinis and cut 4 discs of ham. Finely chop up the bits of ham that are left over and mix in the crème fraiche or cream cheese. Place a disc of ham on each of the four buttered blinis, spread half a teaspoon of marmalade on each ham disc, divide the cream cheese and ham mixture and place a dollop in the centre of the marmalade. Scatter a little chopped sage on each lump of cream cheese and finally a very light sprinkle of freshly ground pepper.

Irish Soda Farl
(Soda Bread)

A very good bread for serving on the side with jams and marmalade.

This is not only an integral part of the 'Ulster Fry' (page 42) – a Brunch which is a heart murmur on a plate – but also a very good bread for serving on the side with jams and marmalade; a delicious morning bread and quite simple to make – no proving or 'knocking back'. One of the important ingredients is Buttermilk; this can be difficult to get hold of and there isn't an alternative, unfortunately.

Pre-heat oven 190°C; 375°F; Gas Mk. 5.

Sift all the dry ingredients into a large mixing bowl. To ensure you have mixed the bicarbonate of soda all the way through; sift it twice. Make a well in the centre of the flour and pour in three quarters of the buttermilk and gradually stir in the flour. Stir the mixture in the middle of the well with your fingers or a spoon and gradually draw in the flour until a dough forms. If the dough is too dry, add more buttermilk until the dough is soft and just a little tacky. Turn out onto a floured surface and knead for about 30 seconds, no longer. The Buttermilk will react with the Bicarbonate of Soda to make the bread rise.

Form the dough into a round loaf (about 20cm – 8 ins in diameter) place on a non-stick baking tray and cut into four quarters with a sharp knife – not quite all the way through or you will harm the tray. Brush with the melted butter mixed with butter milk and place into the oven and bake for 30 minutes. Brush some more butter and buttermilk after 15 minutes baking.

Check that the bread is baked by putting in a wooden cocktail stick and checking it is clean when you take it out. If it needs further baking, put back in the oven for a further ten minutes. If the top is brown, cover the loaf with foil.

To serve; tear the bread apart at the seam. Slice, toast or fry – pop an egg on top.

For a loaf:
500g (just over a pound) plain flour.
1 teaspoon granulated sugar.
1 teaspoon salt.
1 teaspoon Bicarbonate of Soda.
225 to 300ml (over ½ pt.) Buttermilk.
25g (1oz.) Melted butter mixed with
3 tablespoons buttermilk.

Egg White Omelette
with Wild Mushrooms
(V,GF)

if you have a delicate stomach, or slimming, this is the Brunch for you.

I had this at a very smart Hotel in New York. I had never heard of anything so decadent as an Egg White Omelette but it was light and very easy on the tummy - if you have a delicate stomach, or slimming, this is the Brunch for you. Egg whites have some protein, no cholesterol or fat and there are about 16.7 calories per egg white. I think I am right in saying that it is the only alkaline food product we eat!

For each person:

You will need a small non-stick frying pan and a metal (even better; copper) whisking bowl, a glass one will do but not plastic! Whisk up 4 whites with a teaspoon of water until the egg whites are quite fluffy but not so it is meringue consistency. Don't season – you should season after cooking with a little ground pepper.

Heat up a **couple of tablespoons** of extra virgin olive oil in a frying pan and fry **a handful** of whole wild mushrooms. Turn the mushrooms out after lightly cooking and then season with a little salt and pepper. Wipe out pan with kitchen paper.

Heat up another tablespoon more of olive oil, in the frying pan and then pour in the egg whites. With a folk, stir the egg white whilst gently shaking the pan until the egg has the consistency of runny scrambled egg white, then take out the fork. Try not to scrape the bottom of the pan with the fork too much (it doesn't do the non-stick much good). Allow the egg to cook until you can see the sides turning brown when you lift the edges.

Take the pan over to a hot plate, tip the pan up so that the omelette slides out and as it slides out, flip over the top edge and fold the omelette in half with the fork. Arrange the mushrooms to the side and sprinkle with chopped chives and parsley.

You could also serve this omelette with 'Salad with Fruit' (page 13), it would, therefore, be best to fry with groundnut oil or vegetable oil.

Eggs Hussarde

This is a New Orleans version of Eggs Benedict, made famous at Brennan's Restaurant in New Orleans. The breakfast menu there is a vision of various eggs, placed on lots of different things like artichoke hearts or flaky pastry and all – it seems – covered in Hollandaise sauce or cheese! This dish has a lovely sauce called 'Marchand de Vin Sauce' - echoes of New Orleans' French origins. I have based the recipe on the one from Brennan's restaurant. I have had to adapt it, quite a bit, to British tastes and measurements. This is one of my favourite Brunches.

Melt the butter in a large saucepan over a medium heat. Fry the onion, garlic, and spring onions, for 5 minutes, stirring all the time. Add the minced mushrooms and ham; stir for another 3 minutes over a lower heat. Gradually sprinkle in the flour stirring all the time for another 4 minutes, then stir in the Worcester Sauce, wine, beef stock, thyme and bay leaf – simmer the sauce for at least an hour. Just before serving, add the chopped parsley and the seasoning. Take out the Bay leaf.

Put into a cold bowl; a tablespoon of the reduced vinegar and add a tablespoon water, the egg yolk, salt and pepper, put the bowl over simmering water (don't let the water touch the bowel), with a hand-whisk (electric hand-whisk would be better), whisk the egg mixture to a creamy consistency – this will take about 5 minute of continuous whisking! Now, whilst continuing whisking, gradually add the warm clarified butter. Make sure the water in the pan is at a slow simmer and whisk until the sauce is like thick cream or a light mayonnaise. Keep warm in a bowl over some hot – not boiling, water in a saucepan.

For the rest of the dish:

Poach two eggs to a soft consistency. Warm up the slices of ham. Cut the English Muffin half and toast. If you are fortunate to have an Aga, toast the muffins in the hob-toaster. Once you have everything prepared, you are ready to serve up the Eggs Hussardes: On two hot plates, place half a toasted muffin on each plate and cover with slices of the warm ham. Spoon on about a dessertspoon of the hot Marchand de Vin Sauce – not a huge spoonful, just enough to cover the ham, then put on a poached egg and cover with about a tablespoon of Hollandaise sauce. Serve.

At Brennan's Restaurant you get 2 Eggs Hussardes per person! and served, not on English Muffins but on something called a 'Holland Rusk' - not dissimilar to what we gave our children to teeth on in the old days.

For 4 people:

2 English muffins sliced in half.

4 slices of good un-smoked, air-dried ham.

4 tablespoons 'Marchand de Vin Sauce' (see below).

4 eggs.

4 tablespoons Hollandaise sauce (see below).

For 'Marchand de Vin' Sauce:

100g (4oz.) butter. This may sound a little rich but it is authentic. You could use 6 tablespoons of extra virgin olive oil if you feel the arteries clogging up!

100g (4oz.) onion.

2 cloves crushed garlic.

50g (2oz.) (about **4**) spring onions, remove the root – use the green bits as well.

The best way, I find, is to put these last 3 ingredients into a food processor and to finely chop or mince.

75g (3oz.) brown mushrooms - minced.

50g (2oz.) un-smoked ham - minced.

40g (1¾ oz.) plain flour

2 tablespoons Worcestershire sauce

400ml (13 fl.oz.) beef stock.

100ml (4 fl.oz.) red wine

2 teaspoons dried thyme.

1 bay leaf

3 tablespoons chopped fresh flat leaf parsley.

Salt and pepper.

For Hollandaise sauce: a sauce blender or hand electric whisk is vital for this sauce.

250g (8oz.) clarified butter – melt un-salted butter extremely gently until the milky solids form in the bottom of the pan and you can pour off clear melted butter.

2 tablespoons white wine vinegar. Boil until reduced to one tablespoon.

1 tablespoon water.

1 yolk of egg.

Salt and pepper.

Egg Mimosa

For 2 people:

3 tablespoons softened unsalted* butter.

Two thick slices white bread.

4 large free range eggs - as fresh as possible.

1 small pot Salmon caviar or Saviar – or the real thing - Caviar!

A tablespoon double cream.

4 thin slices of Pancetta or very thinly sliced smoked streaky bacon.

1 teaspoon crushed black pepper corns.

I don't know where this originates from (someone might tell me and I will pass it on). This is a summer, warm morning breakfast for someone you want to impress - a new wife (husband) or the boss and/or a new partner when they stay the night. Fish and eggs always go together so well for Brunch:

Pre-heat the oven to 230°C; 450°F; Gas mark 8.

Nearly melt 2 tablespoons of the unsalted butter. Cut the bread into two 12 to 15cm discs (about 5 to 6 ins) using a pastry cutter or a teacup and a sharp knife. Paint both sides of the bread disc with the butter and place on a baking sheet. Put into a hot oven for about 6 minutes or until the bread is turning brown and quite crispy. Put a disc on each plate for serving

Heat up a frying pan to a high heat, pour in a teaspoon or two of vegetable oil and then the slices of Pancetta. Fry until quite crisp, keep warm.

Lightly scramble the eggs – melt the third tablespoon of butter in a non-stick pan. Whisk the eggs and stir into the saucepan, continue to stir the egg over a low heat until it becomes lightly scrambled, still creamy, add the cream and continue until just firm.

Spoon the scrambled egg equally on each piece of bread, flatten the top of each mound with the back of a spoon. Spoon on the Saviar (or Caviar), a little mound in the middle of the scrambled egg. Crush the pepper corns with a heavy kitchen knife or pestle and mortar and then sprinkle over the caviar, place two or three rashers of crisp Pancetta on the side.

You could also serve on Blinis (page 26). A glass of Bucks Fizz (the Americans call it Mimosa – possibly hence the name) or a Peach and Mint Fizz (Page 52)

NB My old dad, who used to be a dairy farmer, told me; unsalted butter is not ordinary butter without salt, it is a butter that has a slightly different churning and production process. It has a distinctively, different taste and is eaten more in southern Europe, not so much in the UK. Personally I do not care for it at breakfast with my toasted soldiers, as seems to be the growing trend in the smarter B&B establishments!

Florentine Eggs

(V,GF)

'veggies' queued up in the mornings, for hot Florentines
- we sold them as fast as we made them!

A nest of spinach bound together with eggs and cheese. We used to have a vegetarian part to our sandwich shop in London and 'veggies' queued up in the mornings, for hot Florentines - we sold them as fast as we made them!

You will need 2 Le Creuset round oven dishes (the type pictured) or 4 round tart cases, (not the type with movable bottoms), or deep, oven-proof saucers. They should be between 10 to 15cm. (4 to 6ins.) in diameter with a good lip around the edge.

Pre-heat the oven 190° C; 350 °F; gas mark 4

Cook the spinach and squeeze out as much water as possible, put the spinach into a mixing bowl. Fry the onions so they do not take on any colour. Mix in with the spinach and allow to cool. Whisk in the egg yolk into the cream and mix in with the cooled spinach, with some salt and pepper. Place the oil or a knob of butter in each oven dish or tart case. Put the tart cases in the pre-heated oven for a couple of minutes to heat the oil or until the knobs of butter have melted. Divide the spinach equally between each of the hot tart cases, make a well in the centre to form a bird's nest, break an egg into each well and sprinkle the cheese over each egg. Put a pinch of nutmeg onto the grated cheese – (I hate nutmeg and I don't put any on mine, but, I am told it is very good and brings out the taste of the egg and spinach).

Place the tart cases or saucers onto a roasting tray and place in the oven on the top shelf for 20 to 25 minutes or 10 to 15 minutes if you like the yolk soft. Take the Florentines, out of the oven and serve with toasted sourdough bread.

For 4 Florentines:

4 tablespoons olive oil (or 2 to 4 heaped teaspoons butter – depending on your cholesterol levels).

500g (little over a pound.) fresh spinach, cooked, with as much water as possible squeezed out – it cooks down to about 300g (11oz.) cooked spinach.

1 finely sliced onion.

2 tablespoons Double cream.

1 egg yolk.

Salt and freshly ground black pepper.

4 large eggs.

50g (2oz.) of grated cheddar cheese or Hollandaise sauce (if you have the time Hollandaise is very 'select' see page 31 or 41 for Hollandaise recipes).

A little **dusting** of grated nutmeg - optional.

Brunch Club Sarni

To produce 4 good-size sandwiches.

1 medium -sliced loaf square white bread (it has to be white!).

50g (2oz) soft Butter.

2 large beef tomatoes, skinned; by putting into boiling water for a minute until the skin blisters and easy to peal off, then sliced thinly.

1 small whole free-range chicken, poached (see below).

8 to 12 rashers streaky bacon, grilled until crispy.

4 to 6 tablespoons mayonnaise.

1 Coz or **Romaine** lettuce, washed.

6 slices of good, un-smoked ham.

6 finely sliced large gherkins.

Salt and pepper.

Poached Chicken:

For a chicken of up to 2 kilos (5 lbs.):

2 tablespoons vegetable oil.

1 large carrot roughly chopped.

1 large onion cut into quarters - skin still on.

1 celery stalk, roughly chopped.

2 cloves garlic crushed.

6 black peppercorns.

1 bay leaf.

A couple of sprigs of various herbs, tied together to make a Bouquet Garni.

1 heaped teaspoon sea salt.

> The Mayonnaise must be home made, the bacon is best crispy and the chicken poached.

A very strange thing to include in a Brunch Book, you might think. But I had some pressure to include a club sandwich from friends Hugh and Sarah, who insist it is, certainly, an essential part of their Brunch on a Sunday Morning. Even if you don't regard this as a Brunch – it is, possibly, the best way to do a Club sandwich for a picnic, a desk lunch or even a 'Latefast' (something for the early hours of the morning). The Mayonnaise must be home made, the bacon is best crispy and the chicken poached. I used to have a sandwich shop in the City of London and we always poached the chicken as it kept the flesh very juicy.

In a big saucepan, with a lid, put in the oil and the vegetables fry for 5 to 10 minutes, over a high heat stirring a few times. Allow the onions to brown a little. Add the Bouquet Garni, peppercorns and the chicken – whole, cover with hot water, ensuring the cavity in the chicken fills with water. Put on the lid, bring to the boil and simmer for 15 minutes. Remove the heat and leave the chicken in the water with the lid on for at least 45 minutes. When it is cool put the whole lot in the fridge until you need the chicken.

You can leave the chicken in the stock overnight. Take the chicken out of the stock, strip off any skin and throw it away. Take the meat off the bones and put the bones back into the stock. You can use the stock again for poaching within a day or two as long as you keep the stock cold in the fridge or you could boil it up and freeze it.

To construct each Club Sarni: Toast 3 slices of white bread. Butter 2 slices. On the first buttered slice; lay 3 or 4 sliced of tomato, then take some chicken meat and pull apart into thin shreds – I prefer the chicken to be shredded rather than sliced. Now put on two or three rashers of crispy bacon, spread some mayonnaise of a second slice of bread and press it – mayo-side down - onto the bacon. Spread some more mayonnaise over the other side of the second slice and cover with a leaf or two of Coz lettuce, cover the lettuce with a slice of ham, then sprinkle some sliced gherkins over the ham. Season with salt and pepper and put the other buttered slice on top. Put a long cocktail stick through each sandwich quarter, so that it does not all fall apart when you cut into quarters (4 triangles). Put an olive on each protruding stick so 'Health and Safety' don't give you a hard time with pointy sticks getting stuck in people's mouths!

Oyster Po'Boys

One of the popular Cajun sandwiches from New Orleans. Possibly, from the French phrase 'pourboire' meaning a 'tip' or a drink, not for a waiter but for the stroppy wife who has been waiting up all night for her gambling husband! For a few cents you could buy a Po'Boy as you lurch your way home - oysters are cheap in the southern States of America. This is a very good 'Latefast' or Brunch sandwich - it is said to have aphrodisiac properties!

Firstly; put the batter flour, cornflour and salt into a sieve and sift into a largish mixing bowl. Put all the batter ingredients into a fridge to get very cold: This is a trick that my friend Rick Stein tells us to do to ensure a crisp batter.

Pre-heat the oven to 230°C; 450°F; gas mark 8

Slice the French Bread nearly all the way through, lengthways and pull out the flesh - leaving a little bit of the white flesh, about 1 cm (¼ inch). Brush the insides of the loaf with the melted butter and place in the oven on a baking tray for 5 minutes or until crisp and golden inside the loaf, allow to cool a bit. Spread the mayonnaise over the inside of the baguette and lay the shredded lettuce into the bottom half of the baguette.

Pre-heat the oil so it is quite hot (not smoking hot).

Make the batter just before you are going to serve. Take all the ingredients out of the fridge, make a well in the flour and break in the cold egg and then whisk in the soda-water, whisk a few times - it does not matter if there are a few lumps and it does not need to rest. Get the oysters out of their shell, dust them with the seasoned flour, then dip each oyster in the batter (it will coat the oyster only thinly) and drop the battered oysters into the hot oil. Fry for 3 minutes then put onto kitchen paper. You might have to do this in three batches so, keep the cooked oysters warm.

Arrange the brown oysters onto the shredded lettuce, sprinkle the capers over the top and lightly dust with the cayenne, press the halves together, cut into 2 or 4 and serve hot immediately, wrapped in a napkin.

I can remember eating something similar in Marseilles, when I was youth travelling around France. It was being sold out of a van in the early hours of the morning on the dockside and, ever since I have enjoyed this for breakfast. They put capers in with their Po'Boy - but they called it something else - I can't remember what it was called but it was magic.

For 2 to 4 sandwiches depending on greed:

1 French Bread long loaf (not the thinner French Baguette).

50g (2oz.) melted butter.

4 tablespoons mayonnaise.

4 Coz or **Iceberg** lettuce leaves, shredded.

12 to 15 Pacific large oysters (or native, smaller and tastier Falmouth or Kentish oysters – they are quite expensive and you would need about 24 - get your fishmonger to open them). Or you could also use about 30 little Queen scallops).

2 tablespoons plain flour seasoned with: 1 teaspoon of each: salt, white pepper and ½ teaspoon paprika.

For the tempura batter:

200ml (7fl.oz.) soda-water (sparkling water is ok but is not quite fizzy enough).

1 egg.

100g (4oz.) plain flour.

50g (2oz.) cornflour.

½ teaspoon salt.

Vegetable oil for deep-frying.

1 tablespoon capers (optional garnish).

A dusting of cayenne pepper.

Carne Picada Burritos
(Spicy Beef)

You could make this well in advance and heat it up in a boat galley or on the prairie or in your garden in Sussex.

For 2 to 4 hungry cowboys- this produces 4 Burritos:

An onion, finely sliced. (I like to slice them from the pointy-end to the root-end, with the root cut out).

2 to 4 Jalapeño or green chillies, de-seeded and chopped (depending how hot you like it – 2 is just a hint of hot).

A little vegetable oil.

450g (1lb.) rump or rib eye steak cut into about 1cm (half inch) thick strips.

½ teaspoon cumin.

2 beef tomatoes, quartered, remove the seeds, and then chop the flesh into cubes.

2 crushed cloves garlic.

Salt and pepper.

4 tortilla flat bread, warm them just before serving.

4 eggs, scrambled.

A Tex-Mex Brunch. This is a hot and spicy breakfast that is best served in the Summer Al-Fresco. A friend of ours, from New Mexico, made this for our breakfast one summer's morning in Sussex – we sat outside and gorged on these spicy wraps with mugs of black coffee. It is a wonderfully hot and spicy dish and jolts one into action, especially if you had rather a 'good' night before. This is another 'camp fire' type breakfast. You could make this well in advance and heat it up in a boat galley or on the prairie or in your garden in Sussex.

Fry the onions and chillies for 5 minutes in a saucepan with a cover, stirring every now and then so that the onions do not colour too much. Remove from the saucepan and put to one side. Fry the steak strips for 2 minutes with the cumin and then add the fried onions and chillies, the tomatoes and the garlic. Season well and cook for 5 minutes over a medium heat.

To serve, lay one warm tortilla bread on each hot plate. Place a couple of tablespoons of Carne Picada down the centre of the bread, leaving a gap at one end. Spoon on some scrambled egg. Fold the piece of bread, where you have left a gap, over the mixture, then, fold over one side then the other, over the mixture so it is in a pocket of bread. Technically, you have created a sandwich, or 'wrap'. Serve hot immediately, its fantastic! Have a mug of steaming coffee (it has to be black – cowboys don't seem to use milk for some reason) and a huge napkin as you will get quite messy.

Texan Steak N' Eggs
with Potato Hash Cake
(GF)

I like to fry steak rather than grill; it seals in the juices quicker. A trick to frying steak to your liking is by prodding the steak with your forefinger, then the fleshy bit of the thumb muscle on your hand – that is 'Blue to Raw'. Now, put you thumb onto your forefinger and prod the steak, then the 'fleshy bit' – and that is rare. As your thumb touches each finger, up to your little finger, the 'fleshy bit' gets harder and harder and is about the same as the degrees of well-doneness of the steak: Fore-finger –rare; middle finger – medium; ring finger – medium well; little finger well-done or ruined (in my view).

Steak and eggs are a typical Cowboy-style breakfast. I love steak for breakfast, in particular, Rump steak; it has a lot of taste and is the better steak to fry. Imagine waking up in the Texan wilderness, slapping half a cow onto a 'skillet' over an open fire, and serving it up, topped with a few fried eggs and lashings of tomato ketchup listening to the Coyotes baying in the distance and the screech of a Bald Headed Eagle overhead. Unfortunately you are not likely to be able to have delicious Potato Hash Cakes if you are out in the desert!

Preheat the oven 230°C; 450°F; Gas Mark 8

Grate the potato onto a clean tea towel and sprinkle with the salt. Mix the salt in with the potato and leave for it to think about life for a couple of minutes. The salt will draw out the moisture. Put the beef dripping into a small frying pan over a medium heat. Whilst the pan is heating up, fold the edges of the tea towel over the potato; twist the ends of the tea towel clockwise one end, anticlockwise the other end to form a towel-cracker. Keep twisting until all the potato juice is squeezed out of the grated potato. Squish it with your hands if you are strong enough. If you have squashed as much of the juices from the potato, turn the potato out into a dry bowl, add ground pepper, egg, crème fraiche, spring onions or chives and mix it all up. Increase the heat under the frying pan, place two chef's rings in the pan (or two empty food tins with the top and bottom removed) and fill each ring equally with the potato mixture. Press the mixture into the rings. Fry for 2 minutes or until it browns. Push the cake, out of the ring (if they stick a bit, run a knife round the inside of the ring), and turn the cake over and brown the other side. Now put the cakes onto an oiled or non-stick baking sheet and bake in the oven for 5 minutes until golden brown. Keep warm for the steak. If you allow the cakes to cool after the frying stage, you then heat them up again in the oven for 10 minutes, they will be crunchy on the outside and fluffy in the inside.

Serve with a couple of fried eggs and the Potato Hash Cake.

For the Potato Hash for 2 people:

150g (6oz) peeled and grated potato.

½ teaspoon salt.

A couple of grinds of the pepper mill.

1 egg

1 level tablespoon crème fraiche or clotted cream.

2 tablespoon chopped spring onions – green bits as well or fresh chives.

1 tablespoon beef dripping or vegetable oil.

You will need 2 to 4 Chef's Rings about 2¾ inch wide by 1½ inch deep (7cm x 3.5cm).

Ham and Egg Strata
A Brunch Casserole

If you want to make it richer, sprinkle some cheese in with the ham and some chopped spring onions.

For 4 people:

4 thick slices white bread, crusts removed, cut into 2cm (½ ins) cubes.

150g (6oz.) thick-sliced and diced, smoked or un-smoked good boiled ham.

1 tablespoon each: chopped fresh sage and chopped parsley (2 teaspoons of each dried).

5 large eggs.

100ml (4fl.oz.) of full-fat milk (don't use semi-skimmed).

100ml (4fl.oz.) soured cream.

1 teaspoon English mustard.

Salt and pepper to season.

America has made a science of breakfast and Brunch. One of more peculiar dishes they serve up is a 'Breakfast Casserole' – so called because it is cooked in a casserole. I have refined it a little as an authentic American Breakfast Casserole is very rich – too rich for even me! You will love this Brunch - simple but different.

Make the night before. You need a small buttered, deep casserole or oven-proof Pirex dish at least about 850ml to 900ml (1½ pts).

Place half of the bread cubes in the bottom of the buttered casserole. It is best to use dry, old bread – a very good way to use up old bread but not if it is starting to grow green bits! Sprinkle over the diced ham and then the herbs. Cover with the rest of the bread cubes.

Whisk together the eggs, milk, cream and the mustard, seasoning. Pour it all over the bread and ham and cover with cling-wrap, place in the fridge over-night or for at least 2 hours.

Pre-heat the oven 190°C; 375°F; gas mark 5

Place the casserole in the oven on a baking sheet and bake, uncovered for 40 minutes. Let it stand for 10 minutes before serving.

If you want to make it richer, sprinkle some cheese in with the ham and some chopped spring onions – not to my personal taste.

Ham and Onions
(GF)

I enjoy this with a fried duck egg; the richness of the duck egg is cut through with the sharpness of the onion.

This is a lovely cold Summer Brunch and also a very old breakfast dish. I first had this Brunch dish when I was invited to Brunch organised by a group called 'Slow Food of Cornwall': They are dedicated to everything that is not 'fast food' and they have wonderful Brunches at lovely stately homes in Cornwall. You can see details about 'Slow Food' at the end of this book.

Heat the oil in a saucepan (with a lid) and stir in the whole peeled onions (if they are quite big, cut them in half). Put on the lid and 'sweat' the onions over a gentle heat for 10 minutes. Add the sugar and season, cook very gently for 30 minutes. Add the Balsamic vinegar and the chopped herbs, bring to the boil and cook for a minute, stirring gently a couple of times. Turn the onions and the sauce into a bowl and allow to cool.

To serve: Spoon out the cooled onions and its sauce onto a plate, lay the ham in folds to one side of the baked onions. I enjoy this with a fried duck egg; the richness of the duck egg is cut through with the sharpness of the onion (very cheffy talk!).

For 2 people:

2 tablespoons extra virgin olive oil.

375g to 400g (14oz.) small peeled shallots or onions (shallots are sweeter). Don't top-and-tail too much when peeling; keep as much of the stalk-end intact to hold the onions together.

1 tablespoon Demerara sugar.

Seasoning.

4 tablespoons balsamic vinegar.

A heaped tablespoon each: chopped fresh thyme or oregano and parsley.

175g (6oz.) air-dried, dry-cured ham like Denhay West Country Ham or Prosciutto Parma Ham

French Toulouse-style
Skinless Sausage - Saucisse de Corbet

The butcher asked if I could call the sausage after the town he lived in – he was very disappointed when I told him it was impossible.

For 12 Saucissons:

225g (8oz) dry-cured belly pork like Italian Pancetta or French 'Lardons'.

225g (8oz) lean pork meat like a leg or loin of pork.

110g (4 oz) beef suet. This is to make the sausage juicy; if there is lots of fat on the belly pork, reduce the amount of suet by half.

75g (3oz) white breadcrumbs.

½ a teaspoon each: salt, garlic salt and ground white pepper.

1 tablespoon granulated sugar.

100ml (4fl.oz.) full red wine, preferably French.

A tablespoon of fresh chopped parsley or **2 teaspoon**s of dried.

I like to put **a pinch** of Ground Bay in the mixture but it is virtually impossible to find! If you can get it, put in a pinch (and perhaps you can send a little to me!)

A skinless sausage so, easily home made, but with more of a French influence. In fact the recipe came from a 'Boucherie' in a southern French town, near where my father now lives in his dotage. The butcher asked if I could call the sausage after the town he lived in – he was very disappointed when I told him it was impossible; mainly because he lived in the charming Gascony town of 'Condom'! So I have called it after my father's house. I have had to adapt this quite a lot as it is impossible to find Saltpetre in the UK and the French cure bacon slightly differently.

Mince or finely chop the meat. The typical Toulouse sausage has course minced meat, so, if you have a big mincing dye for your mincer, all the better, otherwise, chop it up by hand as small as you can, but not too small.

Put all the ingredients in a mixing bowl and mix together thoroughly. The best way is to 'squidge' the mix through your (washed) hands. Ensure you get it all mixed together, then divide the mix into 12 (about 60g – just over 2 oz.) lumps. Kneed each lump of mix a little and then shape into a sausage about 10cm long by about 2 cm thick (4 ins x ¾ ins).

Fry or grill the sausages only after they have rested in the fridge overnight or at least 2 hours. Cook them slowly over a moderate heat for about 10 to 15 minutes. Serve them the Provençal way; hot, in a roll with a little olive oil and sliced tomatoes – or just with an egg.

Brunch on a Stick

A very simple Brunch that you can prepare the day before. All you need to do is light the bar-b-que in the morning and put on the kebabs. Keep an eye on these kebabs; I managed to set fire to some I was cooking when I was not looking and filled the whole neighbourhood with smoke, one still Sunday morning. These kebabs can also be cooked under the grill – possibly safer for the neighbourhood!

Put the bread cubes into a bowl and pour over the olive oil and seasoning. Mix thoroughly so that the oil covers the bread cubes. Thread the cubes of bread (put the skewer through the crust for some stability,) cheese, sage leaf, ham, sausage, another sage leaf, whole cherry tomato and another cube of bread on each skewer then, if you have room, repeat the combination. You can do this the day or evening before to save time or a sleep-in. Light the bar-b-que and wait until the flames have died away and just the embers are glowing.

Melt the oil, lemon juice and butter mixture and brush some over the kebabs. Put the kebabs onto the bar-b-que and keep an eye on them. They will need turning quite a lot and keep an eye on the cheese. Keep basting with the oil and butter mixture. The kebabs will be ready when the bread has turned brown and the cheese has slightly melted. Slide off the skewer onto the plate. The tomatoes are likely to burst if you put too much pressure on them. Serve with Scrambled Egg OR:

Serve with Mock Hollandaise Sauce (Low Cholesterol):

300ml (1/2 pint) Low Fat Mayonnaise
1/2 teaspoon prepared English mustard
2 egg whites
Salt and freshly ground pepper
2 Tablespoons lemon juice

In a small saucepan of hot water, place a glass bowl over the water (not touching the water) into which you whisk all ingredients until smooth. Stirring constantly, cook over medium-low heat until thick.

For 4 kebabs, 2 hungry people.

You will need **4 skewers**, either bamboo ones that you first soak in water for an hour and then brush them with oil, or, 4 metal sewers that you brush with oil.

2 thick slices of good white bread – about 2 cm (½ ins) thick, wholemeal if you are feeling healthy, cut into 2cm cubes with the crust left on. I like to use open textured French bread. Try not to use close textured, plastic supermarket bread.

4 tablespoons good extra virgin olive oil with a pinch of salt and freshly ground pepper.

100g (approx.) cheese - Haloumi Cypriot Cheese is best or Swiss cheese; cut into 2cm (½ ins) cubes..

2 Thick slices of cooked ham, cut into 2 cm (½ ins) squares.

100g (approx) Chorizo sausage – try and get the thin 2cm (½ ins) sausage.

8 cherry tomatoes.

8 to 16 large fresh sage leaves.

2 tablespoons olive oil, a teaspoon lemon juice and a tablespoon butter melted with some salt and pepper to brush over the kebabs.

Ulster Fry

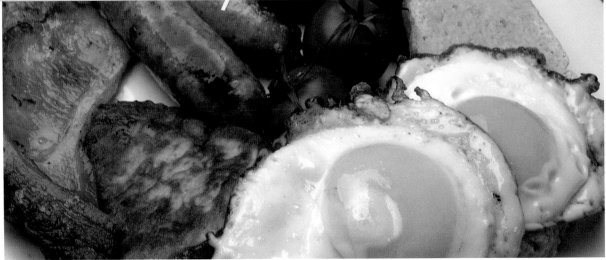

This is a contribution from my good friend, John Smart; an Ulsterman who shares with me a love of Brunch, and an expensive waistline! These are his words, unedited:

2 Eggs

4 Rashers dry cured bacon.

2 Cookstown Pork Sausages [or ordinary, meaty pork breakfast sausages].

2 Slices Potato Bread (from the Ormo Bakery on the Ormeau Road) [I have used an Irish 'BOxDY' potato griddle cake – see page 49 I have no idea what Potato Bread is!]

1 Soda Farl [Soda Bread - Page 29]

3 Slices Black or White Pudding.

1 Large Frying Pan.

Beef Dripping.

1 Defibrillator .

(I was obliged, for reasons of research, to eat an Ulster Fry and found I did not need to eat again for at least two days!)

The bits in Italics and brackets are my thoughts on ingredients and cooking – if any. John is not known for classic cookery, and measurements. So please use this only as a guide.

He says:

"There have been many great contributions to civilisation from the people of 'Nord Iron' but unique on the culinary vista is the "Ulster Fry" of which the "Full English" is but a pale imitation. Food has never been high on the list of priorities for the urban Province dweller... these are people, after all, who grew up with only 2 types of fish, white or brown. "

"Irish minds are on more obvious forms of beauty, for example, no matter where you are in Belfast City you can see mountains, all you can see in England are buildings or flat fields you are not allowed to walk over, depressing even for a city boy like me [John Smart]. Belfast has the Black Mountains and the Antrim Plateau to the North and the Mournes to the South and they are truly dramatic... if it wasn't for the drink you would wonder how this location

could spawn the fools it did. And then there are the Irish colleens... The nation is preoccupied with loyalty, treason, Guinness and the more mobile arts of drama and literature... food is truly only fuel."

"To prepare an Ulster Fry you require: *(this should be for 2 people, however, I suspect John has designed this for only one substantial Ulsterman!)*

Method:

"Fry the lot (in the dripping)... you can butter the Soda Farl rather than fry, but only if Golden Cow butter is available. *(I think you fry the bacon, sausage and slices of black pudding. I would fry the bread and potato Boxdy separately and place the fried eggs on top – well; that would be the English thing to do!)."*

"Serve with wheaten farl, (ordinary white bread 'doorstep-slice') brown sauce, salt and gusto - Large pot of tea... must be Nambarrie, re boiled on the stove. *(Undrinkable thick builders-type tea)."*

"Alternative - for the gourmet/ health freak ... no alternative."

Devilled Kidneys
and Poached Egg

Devilled Kidneys is the epitome of Brunch. It also makes a great supper snack in front of the telly!

Just a wonderful Brunch for us Trenchermen and carnivores. One can imagine arriving down to Brunch at a stately home and running through the chafing dishes with indifferent interest, until, you raise the lid of the Devilled Kidneys, which emits a delicious piquant and savoury aroma. Devilled Kidneys is the epitome of Brunch. It also makes a great supper snack in front of the telly!

Fry the cleaned kidneys (the butcher will prepare them for you) on both sides in the oil and butter for about 3 to 4 minutes on each side, over a medium heat. Take the cooked kidneys out of the pan with a slotted spoon, leaving the juices behind. Keep the kidneys warm.

Bring up the heat and stir in the red wine vinegar and the sugar. Cook for a couple of minutes and then add the rest of the sauce ingredients, leaving the butter to last. Bring to the boil and allow the sauce to boil for only a minute, stirring all the time. Taste for seasoning. Return the kidneys to the sauce and simmer on a very low heat for a minute (more if you like the kidneys well cooked and not slightly pink). It has been known to add double cream to the sauce at this stage but I find it makes it far too rich – I leave it to you.

Poach the eggs. Place a slice of crispy fried bread on each plate. Just before serving the kidneys, stir in the chopped parsley. Equally spoon out the devilled kidneys onto the centre of the fried bread, with a little sauce. Lay a poached egg on the top, dust some cayenne pepper over the yolk and serve immediately.

For 4 people:

8 prepared lambs kidneys, cut in half and cored.

25g (1oz.) butter and a drop of oil.

A little cayenne pepper.

For the sauce:

100ml (4fl.oz.) Red wine vinegar.

2 tablespoons granulated sugar.

1 tablespoon Worcestershire sauce.

1 teaspoon English mustard.

½ teaspoon paprika.

½ teaspoon salt.

Freshly ground pepper.

25g. (1oz.) more butter.

(2 tablespoons double cream – optional).

To serve:

4 thick slices white fried bread; fry and then leave in a warm oven on kitchen paper - the slices will become quite crispy.

1 tablespoon fresh chopped parsley.

4 large eggs poached. Or 4 small duck eggs, also poached.

Cayenne pepper.

Sausage, Bacon and Egg Terrine

To serve 12:

400g (14oz.) un-smoked streaky bacon – at least 18 long rashers.

600g (1¼ lbs.) Sausage meat.

1 teaspoon each: White pepper and salt.

2 teaspoons each: Dried Sage, Dried Thyme.

1 heaped tablespoon chopped fresh parsley.

50g (2 oz.) ready-to-eat dried apricots. Chopped into quarters.

50g (2 oz.) ready-to-eat pitted prunes. Chopped into quarters.

3 small eggs – put into cold water, brought to the boil, boiled for 6 minutes, then plunged into running cold water. The yolks will be a little soft. If you prefer them harder, boil for 8 minutes. Any more and a grey layer will form in-between the yolk and the white. If you have your own hens with very fresh eggs, add 2 minutes.

For a summer picnic Brunch. Served with home-made tomato chutney. I am hopeless at pickles as the process of cooking gets right up my nose – literally! I find Farmers Markets and Women's Institute sell the best delicious chutneys and piccalilli (also good with this Terrine). Or serve with fairy toast (see page 47) or a chunk of rustic wholemeal.

Preheat oven 190° C; 375° F, gas mark 5.

Take a 2lb. loaf tin and line the tin with the streaky bacon: First cover the bottom and the two sides with the bacon, then the ends, leaving a lot of the bacon spilling over the edge, so that you can fold it over the filling at the end. Overlap the rashers along the base of the tin a little.

In a mixing bowl; mix together the sausage meat, pepper and salt, the herbs, and the dried fruit. The best way to mix up the meat is to squidge it through your (clean) fingers until all the ingredients are thoroughly mixed.

Place a third of the mixture in the bottom of the lined loaf tin, be careful not to shift your beautiful streaky bacon arrangement. Inscribe a dent down the middle of the sausage meat mixture. Peel the boiled eggs, be careful not to split them, the yolks are still a little soft. Lay then lengthways along the dent in the meat. Pack more mixture along the sides and in any gaps and then over the top of the eggs and pat down the mixture so that it will fill all the gaps. Fold any ends of the streaky bacon down the side over the sausage meat and then flap the longer end pieces of bacon over to cover the bottom of the terrine. Cover with oiled tin foil and place into a roasting pan. Put the terrine and roasting pan into the pre-heated oven, fill the roasting pan with hot water to half way up the terrine. Bake for an hour.

Remove the loaf tin from the roasting tin of water and leave to cool. When it is cool enough, place in the fridge. To serve, turn out the terrine out of the tin (put it into hot water for 30 seconds to release it from the tin). Turn it onto a plate and slice it into 2cm (½ inch) slices and serve cold, with some whole-grain mustard and a tomato, or what ever you choose.

Smoked Haddock
Fishcakes with Beurre Colbert

Smoked haddock should be a plump fillet of fish, with the merest hint of a smoky yellow, running through the light greyish, nearly opaque flesh.

Smoked Haddock is fast becoming as popular for breakfast and Brunch as eggs and bacon. This is a relatively easy fishcake and can be made way in advance. Smoked haddock should be a plump fillet of fish, with the merest hint of a smoky yellow, running through the light greyish, nearly opaque flesh. Steer clear of the bright yellow stuff. Telly-chefs keep saying don't buy dyed smoked haddock and for some reason it is still sold in the supermarkets, so there must be demand for it! Has it not sunk in that there is little or no benefit to dyed haddock - unless you enjoy a slight metallic taste and, possibly disguised old fish!

Bake the potatoes in a hot oven for about 45 minutes to an hour. When they are ready, scoop out all the flesh into a bowl and mash it up, you will need at least 500 to 600g (1lb.2oz) of potato. Set aside and allow to cool.

Meanwhile; heat the milk in a wide, shallow saucepan or frying pan, with the bay leaf and peppercorns and then poach the fish when the milk comes to a simmer, for 4 to 5 minutes. Allow the fish to cool in the milk – until the fish is cool enough to handle. Remove the haddock from the milk and flake the fish in with the potato, taking care to remove the skin and any bones or peppercorns that might have escaped the milk. Add the spring onions, flour, horseradish sauce and a beaten egg, season well – quite a lot of pepper, not

too much salt – and mix everything together well. Divide into 12 lumps and shape into fishcakes, helped with the dusting flour. It can be a little sticky so keep your hands dusted with flour. Refrigerate until you want to serve them.

Fry the cakes for 3 to 4 minutes on each side in a little oil until golden brown.

Serve with some watercress, and a slice of Beurre Colbert

Beurre Colbert

Pronounced 'colbear' This is a traditional French butter served with fried fish, such as mackerel fillets, kippers or sardines.

Mix the ingredients together with a fork until it is thoroughly mixed. This can be difficult as the butter will slip around the bowl with the lemon juice, but persevere and it will eventually mix into a creamy mixture. Spoon the mixture out onto a sheet of baking parchment paper. Spoon out in a row of lumps evenly across the paper and then smooth the lumps to form a long lump of about 5cm (2 ins) wide. Wrap the paper over the butter until it forms a kind of sausage-shape. Pinch the ends to stop the butter coming out of the ends. Put onto a flat surface in the freezer and leave for at least an hour.

To serve; slice the butter into thick disks and place on the fish or fishcake to melt gently over.

For 6 people, 2 fishcakes each
750g (1lb.11oz.) Baking potatoes.
500g (1lb.2oz.) smoked haddock
500ml (17fl.oz.) full fat milk.
A bay leaf.
6 whole black peppercorns.
2 heaped tablespoons of finely sliced spring onions.
2 teaspoons of horseradish sauce.
40g (1 ½ oz.) plain flour.
1 large egg.
Salt and freshly ground black pepper.
Plain flour for dusting.
Vegetable oil for frying. Vegetable oil makes the fishcakes crispier, however, if you want the cakes a little tastier, use ordinary olive oil.

For the Beurre Colbert
250g (8oz) soft butter.
Tablespoon chopped fresh tarragon.
Tablespoon of very finely chopped shallots – spring onions will do but only if you simply can't get shallots.
The juice and zest of half a lemon.
2 teaspoons cracked red pepper-corns (or the mixed pepper-corns if the red are hard to find). Crack the corns in a pestle and mortar, not too finely.

Eggs Sebastian

For 8 scallops:
(8 or 4 portions, depending on appetite).

For the Sauce Cordelloise:

150ml (5 fl.oz.) ordinary olive oil.

A couple of slivers – with a potato peeler - lemon zest; about an eighth of a lemon.

1 egg yolk.

½ tablespoon lemon juice.

1 tablespoon water.

A little salt and white pepper.

For the finished dish:

A knob of butter and a little oil.

8 thick slices of black pudding, keep the skin on. We in Cornwall use 'Hogs Pudden'.

8 large scallops, in their half shell. Remove the scallop from the shell with a sharp knife. I like to keep the orange 'corral' attached – Americans throw them away for some reason.

Salt and pepper.

10 quail's eggs (you are guaranteed to make a mess of at least two of them!)

Quails eggs on seared scallops on black pudding served with a Sauce Cordelloise (olive oil Hollandaise). This is one of the poshest of Brunches. It is not a very big Brunch, it's but a mouthful, so can be eaten by people with a tiny morning appetite. It will impress and delight the palate. This is what I give to 'food snobs' who think breakfast and Brunch are secondary meals. I pretend that we eat this all the time, every day of the week!

Pour the olive oil into a small saucepan, with the lemon zest, and bring it up to blood temperature. Let it stand at that temperature for at least half an hour so that the lemon zest infuses into the oil. Meanwhile, put the egg yolk, lemon juice and water, with a little seasoning into a glass bowl. Put the bowl over simmering water (don't let the water touch the bowl), with a hand-whisk (electric hand-whisk would be better), whisk the egg mixture to a light creamy consistency – this will take about 5 minutes of continuous whisking! Remove the bowl and saucepan from the heat. Remove the lemon zest from the oil. Now, whilst continuing whisking, gradually add the warm olive oil. Pour in the oil very, very slowly – a mere dribble. Whisk until the sauce is like very thick cream or a light mayonnaise. Unlike a mayonnaise, if this splits, it is impossible to get back! Keep warm by putting a cloth over it, but don't keep it in the oven.

Now for the finished dish – this all happens quite rapidly. Heat up two frying pans – one on a medium heat, one a little hotter but not 'smoking' hot. Line up the plates and the half scallop shells on the plate. In the hotter pan, put in a knob of butter and a little oil to stop the butter from burning. Put in the slices of black pudding or Hogs Pudden. Fry for a minute each side, remove and place on each scallop shell. Now break eight little quail's eggs into the medium hot pan: I do this by gently cutting the shell of the egg with a serrated knife and cracking them into little cups, then pouring them into the pan. At the same time, pour in a little more butter and oil into the hotter pan (the black pudding pan) and put in the scallops. Season them with a little salt and pepper. Fry for no more than 40 seconds on each side, pressing each one, for a second or two, onto the pan. Put a scallop on each black pudding, the egg on the scallop and 'knap' – or lightly coat – each little stack with the Cordelloise sauce. Dust with a little freshly ground pepper and serve. Serve with some walnut-bread toast and orange juice; it is a great combination and very complementary.

Potted Salmon
and Fairy Toast

If, however, you are a believer of no morning conversation, just a newspaper as companion, pot the salmon into ramekins.

Popular dish with both shrimps (better known as a starter for dinner) and salmon. It makes a very good Brunch dish. If you make it into a one large terrine that all have to share, it gets the morning conversation going. If, however, you are a believer of no morning conversation, just a newspaper as companion, pot the salmon into ramekins. Best to be made the previous day or so.

Melt the butter in a large saucepan and add the spices, allow the spices to infuse for a minute or so over a gentle heat, then add the anchovy essence, Worcestershire sauce, a couple of grinds of black pepper, bring nearly to the boil and then stir in the salmon cubes, gently. Take off the heat and allow the salmon heat through for a couple of minutes, stirring only once or twice very gently. You don't want the salmon to break up too much and loose the cubes.

Spoon out the mixture into 6 ramekins or a Kilner sealed jar, press gently down and put into a fridge to solidify. Melt the unsalted butter slowly until you can see the solids separate. Pour off the clarified butter onto the top of the potted salmon. Place the ramekins in the fridge for a couple more hours or overnight.

To serve; toast the sliced bread. Cut off the crusts and slice the slices into two thin slices. Grill the un-toasted side until crisp – you will have to keep an eye on them as they turn to burnt very quickly. Serve the Fairy Toast (you could pretentiously call it Melba Toast) on the side.

I once did this with cubes of salmon and monkfish to great effect. You will need to cook the monkfish first for a little longer than the salmon. You could also use a pint of peeled brown shrimp for a dinner party starter as well as Brunch.

Serves 6 to 8:

100g (4oz.) butter.

A teaspoon blades of mace or a good pinch (½ teaspoon) of ground mace.

A good pinch (½ teaspoon) cayenne pepper

4 scrapes freshly grated nutmeg.

A teaspoon anchovy essence.

A teaspoon Worcestershire sauce.

Freshly ground black pepper.

500g (1lb.2oz.) fresh wild (if possible) salmon, skinned and diced into small 1cm (¼ inch) cubes.

50g (2oz.) unsalted butter for clarified butter.

8 thick slices of white or wholemeal bread.

Smoked Haddock
Brandade and Crispy Bacon

For 4 people:

200g (7oz.) mashed potato.

200g (7oz.) smoked haddock

1 bay leaf.

2 cloves garlic, crushed with the flat of the knife.

1 big slice zest of lemon; just peel off a couple of ins with a potato peeler.

300ml (¾ pt) milk.

Seasoning.

1 tablespoon lemon juice.

½ teaspoon Cayenne pepper.

2 tablespoons fresh chopped chives.

Salt and pepper.

8 to 12 rashers streaky bacon.

4 thick slices walnut bread.

A kind of breakfast pâté. Smoked fish is not only very popular Brunch fare, but also it goes extremely well with bacon. The Brandades are served as 'quenelles' – this is a three-sided, lozenge shape and is very 'cheffy'! You achieve it by moulding a lump of pâté (or ice cream or mashed potato – anything like that) into a neat shape using a couple of tablespoons that have been dipped in hot water for lubrication. It takes a couple of attempts to get the hang of it. Send me an email (hugo@breakfastbook.co.uk) if you run into trouble and I will send you more explicit instructions. But persevere, its worth it for presentation.

Pre-heat the oven 190° C; 375° F; gas mark 5

Make the mashed potato if you haven't got any leftovers and keep it warm. Put the milk in a pan with the bay leaf, garlic cloves, piece of lemon zest and some salt and pepper. Bring gently to a simmer and just before it boils put in the fish. Put the fish into the hot milk to poach for about 4 to 5 minutes. Lift out the fish and remove the skin, don't discard the milk. Flake the flesh into a bowl with the mashed potatoes – keep an eye out for bones. Mix in three tablespoons of the poaching milk, lemon juice, chives and thoroughly mix the mixture into quite a fine pâté. Use the back of a fork. Add more milk if it is too dry. Cool in the fridge for at least an hour. To serve hot; shape the pâté into 8 'quenelles' – a three-sided lozenge shape – with two tablespoons. Place the 'quenelles' on a non-stick baking tray and put in a moderately hot oven to heat through whilst you cook the bacon, or keep in the fridge to go cold. For health and safety reasons, if you are going to serve them warm, you must heat them up to quite hot after allowing them to cool. If you are serving them cold (in the summer for example) make sure you cool them for at least an hour in the fridge. They should not hang around warm for hours!

Put the streaky bacon on a roasting tray that has been brushed over with oil. Put into a very hot oven or under a grill for about 5 minutes. Turn the rashers over and grill or bake for another 5 minutes. Repeat this until the rashers are crispy. Put the crispy rashers onto kitchen paper and dab away any oil. They will keep crispy hot or cold.

Serve a couple of the quenelles to each person, with toasted walnut bread fingers, two or three rashers of crispy bacon and a chunk of lemon. After you spread the toast with the pâté, a little squeeze of lemon, take a bite and then a bite of bacon - fabulous.

Hash Browns
(can be V,GF)

Forget everything you might imagine a Hash Brown should look or taste.

To achieve crispy, flat, tasty Hash Browns for 2 people you need:

150g (6 oz.) peeled and grated potato. Or, for extra fibre, scrub the potatoes and grate unpeeled.

salt.

A couple of grinds of the pepper mill.

A tablespoon beef dripping or goose fat or vegetable oil. Beef dripping offers a lot of flavour, goose fat will make a very crispy Hash Brown and vegetable oil is for those who are vegetarian. Olive oil will not get hot enough to produce crispy Hash Browns.

Forget everything you might imagine a Hash Brown should look or taste. What you buy, frozen in the supermarket or (God help you) get in a certain Scottish hamburger 'joint' – bears no resemblance to a proper Hash Brown. It is so simple to make.

Grate the potato onto a clean tea towel and sprinkle with the salt and mix the salt in with the potato and leave for it to think about life for a couple of minutes. The salt will draw out the moisture. Put the beef dripping into a small frying pan over a medium heat.

Whilst the pan is heating up, fold the edges of the tea towel over the potato; twist the ends of the tea towel clockwise one end, anticlockwise the other end to form a towel-cracker. Keep twisting until all the potato juice is squeezed out of the grated potato. Squish it with your hands if you are strong enough. If you have squashed as much of the juices from the potato, turn the potato out into a dry bowl, add some pepper, increase the heat under the frying pan and put the potato into the frying pan. Spread out the potato so that it is flat like a pancake and fry for about 2 to 3 minutes or until the potato has turned a golden brown lift the edge to check. Flip the Hash Brown over – either cut in half and use a spatula or toss it like a pancake and fry for another 3 or so minutes.

Serve with your favourite Brunch immediately or with a poached egg or anything that has lots of juices to mop up.

Also see:

Potato Hash (V/GF) (page 37)

A thicker and slightly more sophisticated, but not crispy like a Hash Brown; see photo above.

Boxdy
(Irish Griddle Cake) (V)

Perfect with an Ulster Fry (page 42).

It is said:

"Boxdy on the griddle,

Boxdy in the pan,

If you can't make a Boxdy,

You'll never get a man."

May not apply to some of us!

12 cakes:

225g (8oz.) Grated raw potato.

225g (8oz.) Mashed potato.

1 finely chopped fried onion (not traditional but needed, I feel).

225g (8oz.) Plain Flour

1 Egg.

Plenty of salt and pepper

Milk; about **100ml (4fl.oz.).**

Oil and butter for frying.

Mix all the ingredients together with enough milk to make a stiff batter, thick enough to be reluctant to drop from a spoon. Heat a little oil and a knob of butter on a griddle or a frying pan. Drop a tablespoon of the mixture into the hot fat and fry on each side for 3 to 4 minutes. Serve 2 to each 'Ulster Fry'. See photo on page 42. I have added fried onions in the mix as I feel it needed a bit of a lift for our English pallets. I know an Irish cook will be shaking his/her head for this heathenised addition, I sympathise; it's a bit like adding peas to a Cornish pasty, but not as bad!!

350g. (12oz.) King Edward potatoes (peeled weight) peeled and cut small.

25g (1oz.) Butter.

Seasoning.

25g. (1oz.) Butter and a little oil for frying.

1 large Spanish onion peeled and fine diced.

1 leek, cut in half, cleaned and finely sliced.

1 teaspoon dried thyme.

180g (6oz.) finely chopped air-dried ham– like Parma ham or pancetta or cooked bacon.

2 x 85g bags washed watercress – remove the thicker stalks.

Salt and black pepper.

Bubble and Squeak Bacon Hash

I am sure you all know that Bubble and Squeak came from the noise that was made whilst frying this traditional English breakfast in the frying pan. This was created to use up the Sunday Roast leftovers - personally I prefer not to use leftovers but to make with fresh ingredients. I have also changed the traditional cabbage for leeks and watercress. If you just want a lovely Bubble and Squeak (as opposed to the 'Hash') just leave out the bacon and add corn beef. If you want an utterly traditional Bubble and Squeak, I am sure La Delia has a good recipe!

Boil the peeled potatoes for about 20 minutes, drain them and return to the heat to get rid of any extra water. Add the butter and mash the potato, put the mash into a large mixing bowl with a little salt and pepper. Heat up the butter and oil in a non-stick frying pan - the bigger the better. Throw in the onions and fry for a minute; then the sliced leek and the thyme and cook for another 3 or 4 minutes or until they are about to turn brown, then add the chopped up watercress and cook enough to wilt the leaves a little. When they are done remove everything from the pan with a slotted spoon and put into the mixing bowl with the potato – allow to cool.

Add the rest of the ingredients to the potato; ham, leeks and onions etc and mix together; put in the egg last - if the mixture is too sloppy don't put in the egg. You can either make about eight individual bubble and squeaks by putting the mixture into moulds, or chef's rings, in the hot frying pan three or four at a time. Or put the mixture into a frying pan and cook for about 20 minutes. Release the edge of the bubble and squeak with a spatula, place a plate on the bubble and squeak, with a well folded oven cloth over the top of the plate; flip the frying pan and the plate over so that the bubble and squeak ends up on the plate (hopefully it hasn't stuck to the pan). Slide the bubble and squeak back into the pan - uncooked side down for 5 to 10 more minutes.

Serve with a poached egg, brown sauce or piccalilli. It is just as enjoyable cold as it is hot - I love it with cold baked beans but I seem to be the only person in the world who does. Another thing I enjoy is to use cooked Brussels-sprouts and corned beef instead of ham, with a couple of teaspoons of grain mustard.

Fried Worms

As a child, our greatest treat for a late Sunday Brunch was a huge fry-up accompanied by a handful of Fried Worms on the side. This was mainly because the bacon when I was young was always from the butcher, sliced thick, the bacon had a lot of fat and it was dry-cured, not full of water. Now this lovely bacon has come back and it's fashionable, so we can have fried worms again!

Very easy; cut off the rind of thick-cut back bacon, with some of the fat. Arrange the rinds on an oiled baking sheet and put into a hot oven (**230°C; 450°F; Gas mark 8)** for 5 minutes, take out the tray, turn the rinds over and return for another five minutes. You will hear them crackle in the oven. You could get into trouble with the person who cleans the oven as this can make a bit of mess. When the rinds are crisp and blistered, put them onto kitchen paper and put a pile in the centre of the table, they will go quite rapidly. The fat that comes out of the fried worms is wonderful for cooking.

Brunch Drinks

The great thing about Brunch drinks is, it is a little more acceptable to drink alcohol; being nearly mid-day when you sit. The rule of a Brunch drink is it should have properties to inject vitamin C and/or assist with a 'Wooden Mouth' (as the French say) from the night before! Savoury/sweet Smoothies are very fashionable at the moment and here are a couple you will enjoy. My friend David McWilliam, a 'Vigneron' of note in Padstow, gave me the first Smoothie recipe, which will, in my view, shatter all conceptions as to what a Smoothie should be – sweet or savoury. David has called it:

'Bin on the Lash'

For a Smoothie for 2 people:

200ml (7fl.oz.) Orange juice.

2 slices (about 200g – 7oz.) fresh pineapple, remove the skin and the core, chop into chunks.

A handful fresh basil leaves (about 10 large ones) - put a couple of nice leaves aside for decoration. Home-grown basil will be stronger than the forced supermarket pots of Basil. You will need half as much again of the shop-bought basil.

The unlikely addition of Basil to sweet juices sounds incongruous, granted, but it is not dissimilar to the unlikely marriages of freshly ground black pepper with strawberries, chocolate with Chilli Con Carne or Nutmeg with a cup of cappuccino! All must be tried before condemned.

Blitz the ingredient together with a handful of ice. Blend until you can't hear the rattle of ice. It will become a wonderful pea-green. Serve with a straw.

'Scarlet Passion' Smoothie

For a Smoothie for 2 people:

75ml Vegetable juice.

4 Passion fruit – cut in half and the flesh and pips scraped out.

125ml Cranberry juice.

75ml Tomato juice.

Juice of half a lemon.

2 tablespoons chopped fresh tarragon.

2 tablespoons honey (optional).

Vegetable juice, Passion fruit, tarragon and tomato Smoothie. Now this is 'bonkers'!! But so good for you and a wonderfully unusual flavour. It has a rather passionate colour to it – don't get it down your 'Jammies'!

Blitz all the lot together with a handful of ice. Serve with a straw and slice of cucumber floating on the top and, perhaps, a lovely flower. A friend of mine suggested a cooked beetroot instead of vegetable juice would be different. I don't like beetroot but it sounds mad enough to be delicious. I shall however, leave it to you beetroot-lovers to try!

Peach and Mint Fizz

A refreshing morning cocktail. There is something about this drink that makes it taste quite innocent. The combination of innocence and alcohol makes it a very good morning-after-the-night-before drink, like a Bloody Mary. Perhaps I should have called it a 'Peach Mary'!

Put in each tall glass:

2 to 4 leaves of fresh mint, rub them gently in your hand to bruise them, add

A teaspoon of caster sugar, then

A large measure or an **eggcup** of good vodka. Stir with a long spoon to infuse the vodka with the mint and sugar. Put in a straw or two and then fill the glass with ice. Add **75ml (1 and a half measures - 3 fl.oz.)** Peach Nectar, **2 teaspoons** lemon juice, top up the glass with soda water (not sparkling spring water – it is not fizzy enough). Garnish with mint tips (the only thing you should ever garnish with a Mint Tip, in my view!). If you want a non-alcoholic version, use half Cranberry juice, half Peach Nectar.

Tomartini

I thank 'Captain' for coining the name of this Brunch drink. Tomartini is a sort of refined Bloody Mary that uses 'tomato water' as opposed to tomato juice. I got this idea from a 'Home Maker' program on American TV. I was trying to get up one morning after a long flight into Boston, USA for a holiday. I switched on morning TV, to the 'Food Channel' and there she was - Americas answer to Delia Smith; dressed in pink and peach, with a pink and peach work surface and bright green drapes (curtains) behind her, surrounding a fake Georgian sash window with plastic country views beyond. She was showing us how to make 'Tomato Water' "for a wonderful Brunch drink". This demonstration was constantly being interrupted by awful advertisements for cures for bodily inflictions such as 'Acid Reflux' (whatever that is), and Piles – ON THE FOOD CHANNEL??!!! Quite put me off my food – nearly.

Put 500ml (17fl.oz.) tomato juice through 3 thick, coffee filters. Leave to dribble through overnight. If you have room to do this in the fridge, all the better. It should yield about 250ml (9fl.oz.) of Tomato Water.

For 2 Tomatinis:

In a cocktail shaker, put in **6 cubes** of ice, **1 egg cup** full of good vodka, **3 egg cups** of Tomato Water, **2 teaspoons** lemon juice, **3 drops** Tabasco and about **2 to 3 teaspoons** egg white; (add a drop of water to the egg white, it makes it easier to handle). Put on the top of the shaker and shake vigorously for about a minute.

Pour through a cocktail strainer (keeping the ice out) into 2 chilled cocktail glasses with a stuffed olive to decorate. The egg white will produce a froth on top – if it does not get through the strainer, spoon some out onto the cocktail.

Death by Chilled Chocolate!

This is NOT a milkshake and is not a drink for small children (unless they are very, very sophisticated small children – this is possibly a classic oxymoron!). You can find 'Death by Hot Chocolate' in 'Breakfast' - the first book. This is similar but chilled and with the addition of an orange flavour. This drink is very fattening – there is no use trying to gloss over the fact. We slightly rotund people should only have it once a year, on one's birthday – or anniversary – or both.

In a large metal (not non-stick) saucepan, heat the milk and put in the chocolate to melt, break it into little lumps, and do this over a low heat. Using a sauce whisk (as opposed to a balloon whisk), whisk the milk and the chocolate together until all the chocolate has infused (if that is the word) with the milk. Keep whisking for a minute then leave to cook, very gently – not simmering or boiling – for 5 minutes then add sugar stir it in until melted. Remove the pan from the heat and allow it to cool for a minute, then whisk in the Almond essence and orange liqueur.

To serve; put 6 to 8 ice cubes in a drinks blender, pour in the chocolate, doesn't matter if it is still a little warm, break in an egg and whiz up until the sound of the ice has stopped rattling. Serve with a straw and drink slowly – you are only allowed one!

For two people:

50g (2 oz.) Milk Chocolate

50g (2 oz.) min. 70% dark chocolate.

OR 100g (4oz.) real drinking chocolate with at least 50% Coco solids.

300ml (½ pint) warm full-fat milk – you could try semi-skimmed but, in my view, is hardly going to affect the calories!

2 teaspoons Demerara sugar.

1 teaspoon almond essence.

25ml (1 fl.oz.) orange liqueur (optional).

1 large egg – as it is put in raw, not for 'preggers' ladies or vulnerable people (like sophisticated small children!) use a couple of tablespoons of double cream instead.

Index